Goronwy Rees

Writers of Wales

Goronwy Rees

John Harris

University of Wales Press

Cardiff 2001

British Library Cataloguing-in-Publication Data.
A catalogue record for this book is available from the British Library.

ISBN 0–7083–1677–8

Published with the financial support of the Arts Council of Wales

Typeset at University of Wales Press
Printed in Great Britain by Dinefwr Press, Llandybïe

To Rosalind, and Sally (my canine muse)

Contents

Illustrations

Preface

Getting to grips with Goronwy Rees was never easy. The fascinating multiplicity of the man, his diverse professional showings (author, journalist, soldier, businessman, academic administrator), the transition from literary Marxism to Encounter cold warriordom, the looks, charm and intelligence that opened numerous doors and the self-destructive streak that allowed the world to judge him a failure: all make for a complex case; to say nothing of the spying allegations or his troubled relations with Wales. This study, the first of Rees as author, places the writings within a life of startling turns, laying stress on the formative influence of family, the impact of his stays in Germany, and his powerfully articulated responses to unfolding events in the thirties, both abroad and at home. His approach to literature is explored, his aspirations as novelist and the path by which he arrived at his true artistic *métier*, that finely wrought fusion of memoir and social commentary which produced two insightful books of high literary excellence. Nor should Rees's journalism be overlooked: an integral part of his output spanning five decades, it displays an enviable perspicacity and independent-mindedness across a wide intellectual range. This was a mark of Rees, the type of liberal intellectual who, certain of the power of ideas in the world of effective action, sought to influence public opinion on the pressing issues of the day.

Pressure of space has led, inevitably, to the highly selective treatment of Rees's journalism, and comment on *A Bundle of Sensations* and *A Chapter of Accidents* has in turn been influenced by the fuller consideration afforded them in *Goronwy Rees: Sketches in Autobiography* (2001), the one-volume edition of his autobiographical writings I prepared in tandem with this study.

It also needs to be said that, in keeping with the present series, this account puts an emphasis on matters Welsh. Rees published comparatively little on Wales, and next to nothing on Anglo-Welsh literature: which does not make him any less a Welsh writer. This was a point that emerged from the 1961 radio discussion between Rees, Pennar Davies, Emyr Humphreys and Gwyn Thomas on their indebtedness to their Welsh background. The clash of viewpoints was predictable (as was Rees's 'penetrating cynicism'), but what struck Professor Brinley Rees when reviewing the programme was the 'essential cognateness' of all four writers, despite their avowed differences of opinion and outlook. Goronwy Rees, we can readily accept, was as much a man of a place as of an era: the product, as he would insist, of a particular landscape, family and upbringing ('in these we find a sense of actuality, because they have made us what we are').

A number of people have helped me with their recollections of Rees's Aberystwyth principalship: I am most grateful to them all, as I am to Daniel Gruffydd Jones, former registrar of the University of Wales, Aberystwyth, who kindly allowed me to consult the Willink report. I should also like to offer my thanks to Jack Wanger for his insights into Rees the Cardiff schoolboy, to the *Spectator* for placing certain in-house records at my disposal, and to Professor Ralph Maud for reading a draft of this study and making helpful suggestions. My greatest debt is to Jenny Rees, who besides the guidance of her admirable biography, *Looking for Mr Nobody: The Secret Life of Goronwy Rees*, has supplied additional archival material and given up many hours to talk to me about her father. Her encouragement and hospitality have only increased the pleasure of my work on this most gifted and remarkable man.

John Harris
Aberystwyth, March 2001

Chapter 1

GORONWY REES AWOKE TO THE WORLD AT ABERYSTWYTH, IN AN imposing three-storey villa on well-to-do North Road, a little above the town and the cold waves of Cardigan Bay. Rhos (now Pen-y-Geulan) was the manse of Y Tabernacl, the temple-fortress in Powell Street where his father ministered to the Calvinistic Methodists. Though a local man by birth, the Reverend Richard Jenkin Rees (1868–1963) had spent much of his time away, ever since his own father, from a family who worked Ruel Isaf, a farm overlooking Bow Street, moved to London in the 1870s. There John Rees (Goronwy's grandfather) settled in Stepney Green, employed in his craft of stonemason and helping in a dairy business managed mostly by his wife. Their circumstances could be matched all over greater London, wherever Cardiganshire expatriates ran their early morning milk-rounds, the cows tethered in byres behind their shops (and, in the case of the Rees's animals, driven out on to Hackney Marshes for a breath of fresh air). To enter such Welsh premises was to step back into Wales; the language remained inviolate, as did the religion which sustained it. A deacon at Jewin Newydd, the Calvinistic stronghold in the City, John Rees exemplified all the virtues of the faith, not least the belief in education as the surest ladder of success; he and his wife made every sacrifice so that their own gifted sons, Richard Jenkin and his brother Morgan, might attend the City of London School, and, after that, the recently established (and more readily affordable) University College of Wales at Aberystwyth.

Graduating there in Classics, R. J. Rees straightway began a science degree in the hope of a career in medicine. But this was not to be: he came to grief in chemistry, a failure which precipitated a personal crisis resolved at last by his decision to enter the ministry. Looking back at this change in direction, Goronwy spoke of his father as having received a call from God, 'so direct, personal and compelling as to leave no doubt of its authenticity'. His Damascus can be dated to August 1889 when, as R.J.'s scrapbook-journal recalls, 'grief and darkness seemed to be all around my path'. Then suddenly, on a Monday morning,

> In that mountain hollow whose steep sides seemed merciless . . . God shewed me the narrow pass of choice and decision – I went through it, and passing through it, I entered on a valley beautiful in the extreme – along its sides I since have wandered and He has brought me into 'wealthy places'. The path of duty is that of my joy – joy in doing His work in the sacred ministry.[1]

At his side was Apphia Mary James (1870–1931), the nineteen-year-old daughter of Tynrhos, another hillside farm above Bow Street. R.J. had met her while a student at Aberystwyth, and her arrival put a brake on his studies – or so his mother complained. But R.J. held to his choice, marrying Apphia in January 1894, by which time he was pastor of the recently opened English Calvinistic Methodist Church in Ala Road, Pwllheli.

His preparation for the ministry had taken him to Mansfield College, the Congregationalist foundation at Oxford, where he won a First in theology and helped found the Rural Mission Society, an enterprise seeking to revitalize the spiritual life of the locality. So marked was his early dynamism that by the time he left Pwllheli for Cardiff the twenty-six-year-old Rees could be counted among the brightest hopes of his Connexion. Eight successful years at Clifton Street Presbyterian Church, Cardiff, preceded a return to Aberystwyth; he confessed his sadness at leaving the city, remarking that unless his new parish proved a greater field of endeavour he would be even sorrier to have left. The indications are that it never did, even though during his long stay at Tabernacl (1903–22) R.J. regularly strayed from the pulpit into the dangerous waters of local politics (the town council he quickly denounced as 'a chamber of knaves and fools'). Domestically, he and Apphia added to their family; two

Dada: Revd Richard Jenkin Rees (1868–1963). 'All my childhood I had had the comfortable confidence that, as my father's child, I would not fail to be among the elect; it was as if I had been put down from birth as a member of my father's club.'

daughters had been born at Cardiff, while an Aberystwyth-born son survived for just two years. Then along came Richard Geraint and, two and a half years later, on 29 November 1909, Morgan Goronwy Rees. 'Gony' within the family, 'Rees' to his own wife and children, the future journalist and writer owed his first name to his uncle Morgan (R.J.'s younger brother), a medical doctor who died in the Somme offensive evacuating casualties at Thiepval. 'Goronwy' derived from Goronwy Owen, the eighteenth-century poet whose restless life of exile became the stuff of legend. With the name came other of the poet's attributes, for in neither Goronwy did the control and discipline of the writing extend to the personal life.

Goronwy Rees never spoke of his childhood except in glowing terms. He was nurtured in a high-principled, socially minded family with a mother who adored him. The Reeses were elect of the elect: in a town like Aberystwyth ministers of religion enjoyed a respect and authority greater, so Goronwy imagined, than even that accorded university professors; and if this imposed on their children the duty to be whiter than white, the Rees sons and daughters rarely suffered under the burden. There was escape through nature and the imagination, a sense of freedom in the hills and bays, as also in the wealth of reading matter in the minister's house of books and the town's public library. In the mind of the boy, the dream characters in the stories he read blended with the stream of misfits drawn to his mother's back door by her reputation for generosity. The rebellious son of the manse is an accredited Welsh phenomenon, and a convincing case could be made for Goronwy Rees as an instance of the type, but it is proper also to stress the positive legacy of childhood, the Calvinistic inheritance that informed his secular career. One might instance an early self-confidence, a love of books and learning and an enjoyment of exposition and debate, a belief in education and all sacrifices made on its behalf, and a natural spirit of radicalism in the face of society's ills. That Rees abandoned the chapel hardly seems to matter: 'I was brought up a Calvinist', he reflected near the close of his life,

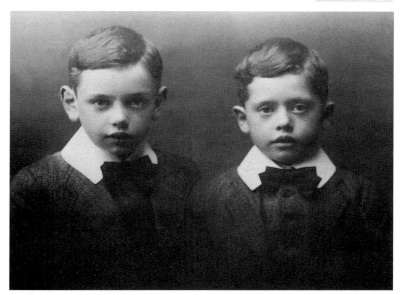

Young Goronwy (right) with brother Geraint. 'You see, Gony was the youngest and Apphia had lost three of the seven children she had and he made her very happy. She was inordinately proud of him' (Margaret Cowell, daughter of Goronwy's eldest sister, Muriel).

'and taught that if one was born of the elect, one never ceased to belong – a doctrine which had strange effects on me . . .'[2]

The Reeses' move from Aberystwyth once more back to Cardiff came in part through disillusionment with events surrounding the notorious Cardiganshire by-election of February 1921. For all his political passion, R.J.'s instinct had been to stand aside from a predictably bitter struggle between the Coalition and Independent Liberals for a rock-solid Liberal seat. Tabernacl was as sharply divided as every other local institution and did not give unanimous support to one of its number, the young barrister Ernest Evans, who carried the Lloyd George banner as Coalition candidate. R.J.'s regard for Lloyd George had long since evaporated, but he came off the fence dramatically in support of Ernest Evans (whose father, clerk to the county council, was a notable pillar of Tabernacl). His entry proved significant, some would say decisive, for he was a formidable campaigner; in any case, Evans defeated the Asquithian Liberal, Llewelyn Williams – though not without Conservative votes and a fleet of Tory cars. A victor in the short run, R.J. came to recognize that he had suffered through such partisan brawling. He should have remained above the battle – as an element in Tabernacl made plain. A minister might speak for his congregation where its viewpoint was unanimous but to take sides in factional conflict only diminished his pastoral authority. Even so, R.J.'s reputation for sagacity and statesmanship – he had brilliantly represented the Connexion before a Royal Commission in 1910 – helped secure his appointment as superintendent of the Forward Movement, a Presbyterian mission evangelizing in industrial south Wales. While distancing itself from socialism, the Movement reached out sympathetically to society's dispossessed; ministers of religion, so R. J. Rees insisted, must be conversant with men as well as with books. They were entrusted with the care of communities; they were the general practitioners of the spiritual world.

The trauma of leaving Aberystwyth ('I felt as if I had been cast out of paradise') was worsened by the shock of Cardiff. 'For my first, yet enduring impression', Rees records in *A Chapter of Accidents*, 'was of the unrelieved ugliness of the city, of its long grey streets and the monotonously repeated vistas of identical terrace houses, the muddy complexion of its stones and the hideously flaring red and orange of its bricks that inflicted themselves on one's sight like a wound' (p. 29). Yet the twelve-year-old Goronwy acclimatized to suburban Roath and to Cardiff High School for Boys. Under the redoubtable J. R. Roberts, the school pursued its high ambitions with scant regard for outside opinion; it was its own world, an academic forcing ground for four hundred pupils from middle- and working-class homes. They were taught by twenty-one masters, some of whom would not have been out of place in university departments. Dyfed Parry, Goronwy's English teacher, had actually been a lecturer at Aberystwyth, while R. T. Jenkins, who taught history, became a distinguished professor at Bangor. Rees later acknowledged the inspiration of these and his other teachers; all were exceptionally qualified and of wide intellectual interests (he would call R. T. Jenkins 'the best teacher of history I have ever known'). It almost goes without saying that at Cardiff, as at similar grammar schools in south Wales, no Welsh cultural ethos was advanced, despite the fact that many of the staff were bilingual and some were the sons of clergymen. Indeed, the paucity of Welsh-language books at Cardiff in the late 1930s inflamed one notable inspector of schools. A teacher remembers the occasion when he and the headmaster, disturbed as they sat in the staff room by a commotion in the room above, hurried upstairs to discover Saunders Lewis scattering the stock of English classics across the library floor.[3] Already those literary classics were becoming for Rees something more important than nationality, for he had awakened intellectually and aesthetically through literature, his key to a world beyond Wales. And despite some well-meaning advice from his Welsh teacher, he would strive to be a writer in English. 'It was as if, in choosing the language of my childhood, I should have chosen to remain a child for ever . . . The trouble was, I supppose, that I wanted to grow up and felt that I could not do it in Welsh' (*A Chapter of Accidents*, p. 34).

From the pages of the school magazine, *Tua'r Goleuni: Towards the Light*, something can be gathered of Goronwy's progress there. On Friday evenings, members of the Literary and Debating Society would gather to hear one of their number speak on a particular author; a voracious reader from the beginning, Goronwy championed Crashaw, Blake and Francis Thompson over favourites like Tennyson and Kipling. In debates he spoke for nationalism and in favour of the popular press. Thought the one 'truly brilliant' man at Cardiff by the headmaster's son T. S. Roberts, an exact school contemporary, Rees naturally picked up prizes, culminating in a school-leaving exhibition, a coveted state scholarship and an open scholarship in modern history at New College, Oxford, commencing in October 1928. New College was his mother's choice; she had spent one summer's afternoon there, sitting in its gardens with her husband, and deciding on the spot that this most beautiful college was the proper place for her son. He took some time to settle there, for despite his prowess in English he had chosen to study history, and later, as he explained, switched to Modern Greats 'in the mistaken belief that philosophy, politics and economics provided the key to the secrets of real life' (*A Chapter of Accidents*, p. 76). Academically he had little to fear, because his preparation had been of the best ('arrogant in the mind' is how the Oxford-bound Rees has been described),[4] but quickly he came to realize that success at university depended on something apart from brain power.

There are two views on Rees the undergraduate – his own and other people's. He described himself as an interloper, on account of his nationality, social background and temperament. New College was a Wykehamist domain, 'the almost exclusive preserve of the English ruling class, a kind of pheasantry in which the products of the English public schools were reared like game birds'.[5] To a Welsh grammar-school boy with little experience of England, and none of its public-school élite, it seemed impenetrably alien. Yet Richard Crossman remembered 'an extremely brilliant and handsome scholar who took Oxford society by storm', and other of Rees's contemporaries were agreed on his enviable assets: his intellectual prowess, his wit and charm, his magical conversation and the Byronic good looks so beguiling to women and to men. A. L. Rowse called him one of Connolly's 'deadly irresistibles', remarking his raven-black curls and violet-blue eyes (they were green to Shiela Grant Duff, Rees's girlfriend of the early thirties). Richard Wilberforce, a year behind Rees at New College, thought him very comfortable among Oxford's intellectual set ('of course I was attracted – enchanted – by him – his looks, his cleverness, his reading – and this never left me').[6]

This Oxford transformation was not achieved without an emotional cost. Shiela Grant Duff has spoken of deep internal

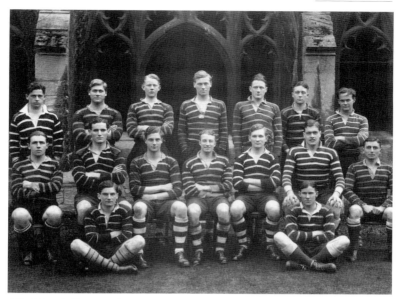

The New College Rugby XV, 1929–1930. Rees stands appropriately at outside left, behind a seated Richard Crossman: 'he used to exasperate me by his assumption that rugby was a matter of brute force rather than intelligence, which offended all my instincts as a Welshman.'

conflicts within Rees, of how complex and baffling he could be, and how he admitted the harm he had done himself by taking on a protective colouring. It was Rees's misfortune, suggests Richard Wilberforce, 'to come, detached, from Wales'; the Wyke-hamists had their school friends and families to support them, and settled intentions regarding their careers. Yet detachment was Rees's favoured position. He sought liberation from national ties, and from personal obligations as well. As he wrote to Maire Lynd, daughter of Robert and Sylvia Lynd and a regular correspondent at this time, 'That people should look to me for advice or depend upon me horrifies me. I like loving people and being friends with people, but being depended upon I cannot bear.'[7] Friends and lovers he found in plenty; there was talk of Rees the cold seducer, indiscriminately amorous: 'an adored and somewhat spoilt young exquisite', in Richard Crossman's words (*New Statesman*, 25 February 1972).

That Apphia Rees had spoilt Goronwy, her youngest and favourite child, was acknowledged within the family. From her unconditional love, as much as from his father's Calvinism, came the belief that he could do no wrong; or that if he did, forgiveness would be at hand. When after graduation this security was snatched away by his mother's sudden death, he could barely express the loss. Nothing remotely as bad could ever happen again: 'Everywhere really I depended on her & I felt whatever I did it didn't really matter.' She validated his every move, even a second-year affair with 'a very beautiful & wild young man'.[8] His father's world likewise lay in ruins; he and Apphia adored each other and had spent their lives together. 'Brave true woman', runs a note in R.J.'s scrapbook, 'unyielding in her courage, reliant in her love, my guardian angel at all times.' For father, as for son, the face of life had changed.

Some thirty years later, speaking of his personality as it emerged, Rees mischievously dubbed himself Mr Nobody. He suggested he had no fixed character of his own, enlisting Hume in his defence, the philosopher who had called into question the notion of a substantive self. But it was Walter Pater who better explained Rees's thinking, or so believed A. J. Ayer, remembering how at Oxford *The Renaissance* had been Rees's golden book (as it had been Wilde's).[9] 'A drift of momentary acts of sight and passion and thought', wrote Pater of our actual experience, famously concluding that 'Not the fruit of experience, but experience itself, is the end.' One had to live in the moment, savouring each passing sensation. Such notions challenged Rees's wish for detached neutrality and the clash of these irreconcilables provided thematic material for the novel he was writing. 'To live as if living itself were the sole important purpose', was his fictional gloss on Pater (*The Summer Flood* (1932), p. 224). In his later years he would claim that these Oxford influences (they would have included Maurice Bowra's brilliant hedonistic circle) profoundly and permanently affected him: throughout his life he continued to feel that the circumstances in which he found himself were purely provisional and transitional – this had militated against any notion of a steady career – and, child of the twenties, he remained an open enthusiast of the pleasure principle. Pleasure, which might not be highly regarded in Wales (except as the accidental product of the pursuit of higher things), was for Rees something to be cultivated for itself.

By 1931, his final year as an undergraduate, the pressure of outside events had begun to be felt at Oxford. In the face of the great depression moral consciences were stirred, so that the pleasure addicts of the twenties became the social radicals of the thirties. Rees's correspondence mirrors the change. In one letter, he claims to be 'infinitely detached and indifferent to the world and all its inhabitants and events', yet the plight of the south Wales miners, witnessed directly at Merthyr, genuinely disturbs him:

> I can't stop thinking about that incredible town. To talk about goodness and beauty and truth when such things exist seems to me complete hypocrisy. All this worries and saddens me, I think, more than my mother's death . . . Merthyr seems to me a complete negation of life. I can't really express its significance . . . What one can do I don't know, but one needn't live as if it didn't exist. That's a sort of final treachery to everything one admires.[10]

If Merthyr proved a significant turning point – it produced a poem of identification with the miners[11] – one must add that his discomposure at this point stemmed also from the lack of any personal career plan. Literature was his obsession; he had published in the *Oxford Poetry* series, the landmark anthologies introducing a lustrous new generation of authors, but literary ambitions did not blunt his critical judgement about his poetry. His novel was a different matter, the book which occupied him compulsively during his final year at New College: 'Writing books is the only thing I'm serious about, and I think mine is good' (undated letter to Maire Lynd [1931]). His letters after graduation speak of the novel's progress and of suitable openings in journalism that might support a writing career. Then, bolstered by a First in Modern Greats, he allowed himself to consider the possibility of an All Souls fellowship.

'If I don't leave Oxford now I shall become as genteel and unreal as everybody else there', he wrote to Douglas Jay in 1931. Jay was different, his Wykehamist brand of socialism, so drearily proper in Crossman, streaked with a personal eccentricity; Oxford might be redeemed by his company, as by friends like Freddie Ayer (another iconoclastic misfit), John Sparrow ('all elegance and style') and witty, attractive Martin Cooper, who later, as musicologist, would join Rees at the *Spectator*. Whatever his misgivings, in autumn 1931 Rees put in for the All Souls examinations. His history paper was shaky, but an outstanding essay on the middle classes impressively retrieved the situation. 'Very surprised & pleased', he confessed to his father, reporting his All Souls success, and even in a family where academic distinctions came readily – his brother Geraint had that summer gained a Cambridge First in law – Goronwy's achievement warranted celebration. It was Douglas Jay (himself prize fellow for 1930) who put it in perspective: 'though he [Rees] has lots of supreme talents which I have not got, he was actually elected for the moderate ones he shares with me and the interest in the truth we both care about.' Rees's looks, mind and manner might have made for social success, but what ultimately mattered was the value and seriousness of his concerns, 'a desire for truth about the most important things and a determination not to be weak or lazy or dishonest in finding it' (letter to Shiela Grant Duff). He had gained the first prize fellowship for 1931, the second going to Quintin Hogg, son of a lord chancellor and a scholar of Eton and Christ Church. The grammar-school boy had triumphed, and in celebration of Rees's fellowship (just three years on from the sixth form), Cardiff High declared a rare half-holiday.

Rees's undergraduate pattern had been to alternate Oxford high life with vacational study at home. Cardiff might be 'very unbeautiful' but being home at 39 Tydfil Place, a stone's throw from Roath Park, was 'wonderfully uncomplicated', the hours of study lightened by walks around the lake in the park. There were family holidays also, in Pembrokeshire and Pwllheli, one of which introduced him to a north Wales cousin by marriage, with whom (as his letters to Maire Lynd during the summer of 1931 report) he fell 'terribly in love': she was 'very beautiful' but 'too simple and good' to connect with a wayward young man from Oxford. 'She made me miserable for two years', confessed Rees, even as he placed this misery at the centre of his undergraduate novel. There could be no concealing the dismal passion: 'The worst we can do to ourselves is to imagine ourselves as we are not.'

Rees in this early period held to a notion of fiction which rejected the moralists and teachers in favour of writers who explored the inner lives of their characters. Turgenev was his master, admired not as Rees would come to admire him, as a profoundly political artist, but as an acute psychological analyst. If Turgenev did little for his confidence, Rees persevered with his own psychological essay, achieving results 'which I can't help feeling very good'. Others thought so too, most importantly Geoffrey Faber, estates bursar of All Souls who, in his role as publisher, kept an eye on Oxford hopefuls. He believed that Rees had promise, and in July 1932 *The Summer Flood* duly appeared under the Faber imprint. The novel is unashamedly autobiographical, with all the charm of a very first book. Rees is cast as Owen Morgan, a vain and temperamental undergraduate who on a family holiday in Llŷn once more encounters Nest, the cousin who has previously rejected him. Owen resolves to ignore her, but over five days in summer all his old feelings return, this time to be reciprocated. Except for a catastrophe at sea, the novel shows little by way of incident, focusing instead on Owen's state of alienation from two opposing social worlds. We glimpse an Oxford of the Bright Young Things, where raw intelligence must always be masked by physical charm, social grace and theatricalities of dress and manner. The gulf is at its widest in the backgrounds of Owen and an Oxford friend, a wild young libertine named Sasha: 'Drunkard, idler, pervert, degenerate – all

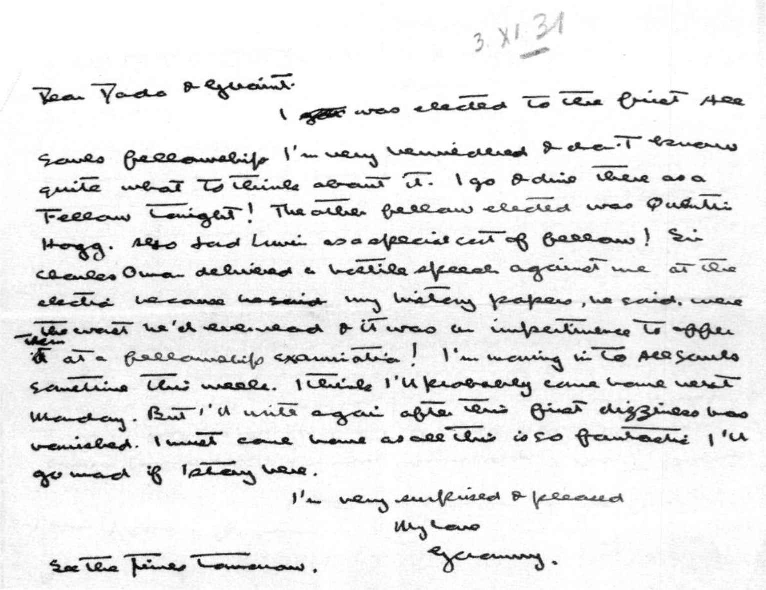

3. XI. 31

[handwritten letter reproduced below]

Dear Dada & Geraint.

        I was elected to the first All Souls fellowship. I'm very bewildered & don't know quite what to think about it. I go & dine there as a Fellow tonight! The other fellow elected was Quentin [*sic*] Hogg. Also Lord Irwin as a special sort of fellow! Sir Charles Oman delivered a hostile speech against me at the election because my history papers, he said, were the worst he'd ever read & it was an impertinence to offer them at a fellowship examination! I'm moving into All Souls sometime this week. I think I'll probably come home next Monday. But I'll write again after this first dizziness has vanished. I must come home as all this is so fantastic I'll go mad if I stay here.

               I'm very surprised & pleased
                   My love
                      Goronwy.
See the Times tomorrow.

[An examination fellow, Lord Irwin (later Lord Halifax, foreign secretary, 1938–41) was re-elected to an honorary fellowship in 1931; Sir Charles Oman, another fellow, held the Chichele chair of modern history.]

Rees writes excitedly home with news of his All Souls success.

these things Owen had thought and been told before' – as indeed had Goronwy of an extravagantly dissolute New College homosexual whose company he kept (thereby earning, as he admitted, 'almost everyone's disapproval, & a good deal of contempt').[12] Against Sasha's corrupting aristocratic bloodline stands Owen's Welsh inheritance, most of all the Calvinist ambition that drove his father to become a minister (as a boy reading Cicero on the back of an east London milk cart). Owen similarly has advanced, not by accident of birth, but through hard-won competitive scholarships. Yet, if Owen belongs to his people, he must break free of their religious obscurantism and the 'affection-ridden' world of the extended family. He breathes a freer air in Oxford – even as he longs for the security of home.

The Summer Flood dramatized another internal conflict, that between Owen's notion of living an interior life and his wish to become more fully the man of action. Made strong by Nest's love, he imagines he yet might take possession of the tangible world, there to play 'the decisive, active part he wished, in the living scene of which now he was doomed to be merely a spectator' (p. 224). (Pater's 'gemlike flame' finds an echo in the image of Owen and Nest as thus far having 'clothed themselves against the perception of life, like one who holds a screen to protect himself against the fire, against the intensity which there is in living itself'.) But such reorientations of personality are dangerous; discarding her puritan certitudes, Nest has now only Owen, 'a fickle navigator to trust for guidance over such strange seas'. And she drowns in a sudden sea storm, seconds after the collapsing mast of a sailing boat splits open Owen's head. He too has deluded himself. At the moment of his transformation, the rejection of the introspective self, 'a curious emptiness possessed him, as if his life depended upon the fears and self-mistrust which now had been destroyed, and as if their destruction had left him with no self at all'. For all its agonies and distortions, that which originates in the self somehow has more reality; it is in the drama of the mind and emotions that he feels most intensely alive.

The frankness of *The Summer Flood* ruffled some family feathers and provoked amusement at Oxford. If the book made too much of adolescent anguish, the critics at large were kind, L. A. G. Strong and L. P. Hartley applauding the way it captured the essence of youth. The *Times Literary Supplement* was also beguiled, almost against its will: 'modest and amiable rather than ambitious and really striking', the novel somehow lodged in the mind. 'Is it the simple fascination of youth in love, or of a setting so local, so strange as almost to be foreign?' Those for whom the setting was native celebrated other virtues, the *Western Mail* remarking how in attempting to penetrate the mind of a young middle-class Welshman the book had extended the range of Welsh fiction. In all, the reception encouraged the author to press on with a second novel.

Chapter II

BETWEEN THE WINNING OF AN ALL SOULS FELLOWSHIP AND HIS acceptance, four years later, of a post with the *Spectator*, Rees was chronically restless and uncertain in his choice of career. In September 1931 C. P. Scott at the *Manchester Guardian* preferred him to Isaiah Berlin for a vacancy as leader writer, a golden opening for any budding journalist but one which Rees, lukewarm at the prospect of Manchester, would not take up immediately. He had spent one undergraduate summer in Silesia, tutoring the son of a Prussian baron, and now he longed for Berlin and Vienna. 'I am very fond of excesses', Rees confessed, and Germany dealt in extremes – in philosophy, politics, and the arts. The culture of Weimar beckoned, 'a restless, disturbing, dialetical spirit' (*Encounter*, March 1969). It was in Vienna that Rees first settled, in the spring of 1932, excited by its intellectual vibrancy and enlightened municipal socialism. Though doomed as a cultural focus, the Austrian capital still attracted visitors from every part of the world. There Martin Cooper studied music under Webern, while Freddie Ayer attended seminars of the Viennna Circle. Rees took lessons in German before moving on to Berlin, where he managed to appear in a nationalist film produced by the giant combine, UFA; Ayer saw *Flüchtlinge* ('Fugitives') in Vienna and was astonished to recognize Goronwy in a kilt, impersonating a Highland officer. At some point in the summer Rees also journeyed to Russia, accompanied by Shiela Grant Duff. The curly-haired, bow-tied Goronwy hardly blended with the Soviet workers, though on one occasion this worked to his advantage: he and Shiela were battling to board a Moscow tram when a soldier suddenly shouted, 'Give way! He's got culture' – and like the waters of the Red Sea the crowd miraculously parted.[13] By the end of 1932 Rees had returned to England, to the *Manchester Guardian* position, but within months he threw in his cards for yet more continental travel. This time he took in Czechoslovakia, with Shiela and Isaiah Berlin as companions; Shiela describes how, on their travels, 'Goronwy and Isaiah continued their long philosophical discussions of which I understood not a word and against which I protested ineffectually' (*The Parting of Ways*, p. 53). Isaiah would become a lifelong friend: he was another outsider, the first Jew to be elected to All Souls, as Rees was the first state-educated Welshman there.

January 1934 saw Rees once more back in Germany, pursuing research into Ferdinand Lassalle (founder of the Social Democratic Party) at the Prussian State Library, Berlin. It became the central experience in his political evolution, but it was the liquidation of socialism, not its founding, about which he now learnt. Hitler was Reich Chancellor of a brutal one-party state whose horrors Rees witnessed at first hand. Setting aside his academic research, he mixed with the outlawed Social Democrats, through them becoming acquainted with a type of political thinking, alien and perplexing, yet at the heart of the international socialist movement; it was devoted, so it seemed to him, 'to adjusting and adapting the events of the real world to its preconceived views of what ought to be, indeed must be if one can penetrate to their deeper reality'.[14] In German socialists it fuelled the conviction that the proletariat was the true revolutionary force; the working classes, once united, would re-emerge in glory to redeem a fallen world. The dialectic of history demanded it. No matter the hunting down of communists and socialists in the streets and cellars of the city – the Nazi terror was but a temporary phase. At some risk to himself Rees helped sustain this illusion, supplying copy for Social Democratic broadsheets run off on a clandestine hand-press, the Left's pathetic response to the torrents of Nazi propaganda. Back in England, he gave up completely on Lassalle and by November 1934 had joined the staff of *The Times* as a home sub-editor. As with the *Guardian*, his stay was brief; in March 1935 he turned his back on the security of *The Times*, dismayed by the paper's support for the policy of appeasement. The parting was otherwise amicable: Rees was grateful for a few months' experience of the newspaper's sub-editing room ('more of a research institution than a newspaper office'). On balance, he felt comfortable in journalism, a generous and sociable world, incestuous and enthralling, though one was 'apt to forget that what one is dealing with is a very thin surface of events . . . the days slip away very quickly until, at the end of a few years, you find that you are incapable of thinking of anything except NEWS'.[15]

Early in 1936 Rees landed the job that exactly matched his talents: he became assistant editor of the *Spectator* at a salary of £500 a year (for a three-day week). Although just twenty-six, he had some experience of leader writing and a range of expert knowledge. Besides a passion for literature and politics, he possessed a technical grasp of economics and a command of foreign affairs that, in relation to Germany, put him in the category of expert. A student of the weekly press of the 1930s has commented on this: the British educated classes knew precious little of Germany, and of those drawn to developments there – chiefly the literary intellectuals – only Rees and Richard Crossman gained editorial posts on the weeklies.[16] Rees knew Nazi Germany, had heard Hitler in the flesh, was acquainted with *Mein Kampf* (several years before its appearance in English), and had studied the activities of the *Freikorps*, those counter-revolutionary patriots of the right who provided the National Socialists with much of their theory and practice.

Sharing the duty of leader writing with the *Spectator*'s editor, Wilson Harris, between February 1936 and August 1939 Rees contributed one hundred and fifty or so lead articles on foreign and home affairs. He became a regular book reviewer (Derek Verschoyle was literary editor) and wrote the occasional signed essay (book reviews were signed, though not lead articles). Taken as a whole, his *Spectator* journalism provides a detailed guide to his political thinking during a momentous decade – and incidentally counters the impression, fostered not least by himself, of his flippancy and indolence during these early years; those who employed him emphasized his professional competence and industry. The *Spectator* might seem an improbable berth for an outspoken radical socialist but, while politically leaning to the right, the journal was decidedly open-minded in its approach to literature and the arts. Wilson Harris, a chilly Liberal pacifist Quaker, controlled editorial policy, and Rees was forced to exercise a degree of self-censorship, at least in his spectatorial role; paradoxically, in his signed reviews he could be more freely himself.

Settled in his Gower Street office, he turned at once to Spain where the forces of the Left had won an electoral victory. As he saw it, the strength of the Popular Front lay in its concrete programme for precise and positive ends; the danger was that the alliance of socialists, communists and anarchists would break on internal questions before these ends were achieved. Then in July 1936 came the revolt of the generals and the outbreak of civil war. Rees put forward the *Spectator*'s position, one which offered full backing for the Republic but made no demand for British military intervention. This was essentially a civil war and, 'Callous as it might seem, the great issues which hang on the Spanish conflict must be entrusted to the courage and endurance of the Spanish people themselves' (7 August 1936). As a concomitant, the Germans and the Italians, who from the outset had aided the insurgents, must be persuaded to remove themselves from the fray. This did not happen. In fact, increasingly effective German air power tipped the military balance in favour of the rebel nationalists. Abroad, such a development hardened policies of non-intervention; if the German Condor Legion could so devastate Spanish towns and villages, what might it not do to British cities should a general war break out? It has been persuasively argued that fear of German air power, more than moral concern at the injustice of Versailles, lay behind the policy of appeasement (of which non-intervention in Spain was a part), and that this was a consensus position embraced also by the Left, whatever its emotional commitment to the Spanish republic. But

Spain figures only marginally in Rees's journalism of the 1930s; he kept his eyes on Germany.

It was over German policy that he and the *Spectator* were most seriously at odds. Writing from Berlin to Shiela Grant Duff in 1934, Rees described the Hitler state:

> Here what seems a nightmare in London is the sober everyday reality: the betrayal and death of every human virtue; no mercy, no pity, no peace; neither humanity, nor decency nor kindness: only madness, shouted every day on the wireless and in the newspapers, spoken by ordinary people as if it were sober sanity: and sixty million people pleased and proud to be governed by a gang of murderous animals.[17]

The Nazis were criminally insane and had to be stopped at whatever cost. It pained him that normally intelligent British people could not understand how profoundly evil they were – on the contrary, admiration for Germany ran deep within the governing classes. From All Souls, and indeed *The Times* (whose editor, Geoffrey Dawson, was a senior fellow), he became familiar with the pro-German arguments: that Hitler's territorial aggression was a legitimate attempt to redress the iniquity of Versailles, and that by acceding to his just demands a lasting peace might be bought. Douglas Jay recalled Goronwy fervently arguing against this position (as did the majority of younger fellows, including Rowse, Berlin and Jay himself). Hitler had gambled against there being any effective outside resistance, either through economic sanctions or military threat; appeasement simply consolidated his position as Führer, sharpened his lust for power and furthered the gigantic build-up of the German war machine. Resistance by the Versailles powers, which at the outset might have stifled the Nazis, could yet reverse these processes by exposing the lunacy of Hitler's ambitions and hastening a system of alliances against him.

In the meantime Britain must be disabused about the nature of the Nazis. How was it, Rees repeatedly asked, that so great and civilized a country should fall for a mountebank genius? Was there something inevitable about Hitler's rise to power, about the processes by which he and the German people came so completely to identify with each other? 'We are a people of faith', declared Alfred Rosenberg, the Baltic pseudo-philosopher, and Rees was inclined to believe him. Rooted in tribal barbarism, Nazi ideology placed a belief in racial purity at its spiritual centre and, as in a new dark age, suppressed that instinct for rational enquiry which had been the foundation of Germany's greatness. Now learning was to be founded not in truth but in blood. Hitler's success lay also in his understanding of the 'little man', and in his voicing of the aspirations of those millions of lower-middle-class men and women who, having endured years on the breadline, accepted the violence of totalitarian methods to overcome the miseries of mass unemployment. They acquiesced in the fanaticism of their leader, in his myth of the Nordic race and his glorification of war. Within the party itself criminals were leading madmen, bemused and drunk on the promises made them. The threat to European civilization was immense, for the Führer was a man to whom all civilized values were unreal:

> what is real are the instincts of brutality and barbarism whose effects can be seen, touched, smelt and easily understood . . . He is ignorant of facts and does not understand theories. One idea is much like any other, and for him words have no meaning but only an emotional propriety. When he says Peace he might as well say War . . . (20 March 1936).

This remained Rees's undeviating position: Hitler should never be taken at his word; he lied by nature, habit and conviction: 'a promise of peace is the nearest he comes to a declaration of war.' In *Mein Kampf* he had supplied a defence of the lie as an instrument of policy and his techniques of propaganda had been stunningly successful: 'one has only to read the correspondence columns of *The Times* to realise that even the most upright men may unconsciously adopt and urge arguments that would never have obtained the slightest credence but for Germany's insistent and insidious propaganda' (19 May 1939).

Though Rees's leaders continued to agitate the apologists for fascism ('such colossal bias is unworthy of your paper'), the *Spectator* generally maintained a policy of appeasement, at least until 1938. The shame of Munich transformed its position, allowing Rees to move more fully centre stage. With new eloquence and authority he took up the menace of imperialist Germany:

> Politics is an art of achieving limited objectives; and precisely because Herr Hitler's objectives are unlimited they can only lead Germany, and the world, into chaos. In their present form they are one of those megalomaniac dreams that have such terrible power over the Germanic mind, and time and time again have brought Germany to ruin. (17 February 1939)

> The discipline he [Hitler] has imposed on his people cannot conceal the chaos he has created. In part, it is the means by which anarchy is turned into a weapon against the outside world; in part, it is the measure of the violence which is necessary to hold a people together after every religious, moral, social and political tie has been destroyed. It was Nietzsche . . . who predicted, half a century ago, that the modern Nihilist would substitute for the social and cultural ties he destroyed the bare, empty, dogmatic, mystical conception of *das Vaterland*; Hitler has fulfilled the prediction to the letter. (21 April 1939)

Rees also rebutted the notion, by 1938 a platitude, that Germany's eastward expansion was natural and inevitable, and that any moves to block it were somehow attempts to encircle her. Not even Germany's own government believed this, no matter how actively it propagated the viewpoint. The only foundation for a foreign policy was a programme of collective security. As the weakness and vacillation of the democracies had encouraged German ambitions, so now a unifying alliance against Nazism was imperative, and one which included the United States and the Soviet Union as well.

Rees's thinking on Russia should be disentangled from his relationship with Guy Burgess and the Cambridge spy ring, an involvement which became public knowledge in the 1950s and darkened the rest of his life. Certainly the young Welsh radical who journeyed to the Soviet Union in 1932 was ready to be impressed. What he saw there dismayed him and served as a counterbalance to the reports and opinions of others. His very first *Spectator* review (13 December 1935) questioned whether *Soviet Communism*, an admittedly impressive study by Sidney and Beatrice Webb, was more a social blueprint drawn up by two sociologists of genius than a picture of an actual society. Rees could not forget his own Russian visit:

> pictures of a street in Leningrad filled with broad unsmiling Mongolian faces, of onion-shaped cupolas on the Moscow line, of a waggoner standing over a starved horse and flogging it as it died between the shafts, of a hospital where flies crawled undisturbed over children's eyelids because the Five Year Plan had not allowed for gauze, of jerry-built tenements run up without plan and without beauty; and not only these absurd images, but a memory of the peasant who knelt down and kissed 'the dear Russian earth'.

Faced with first-hand reports, Rees allowed himself to hope that Stalin's talk of democratization had some basis in reality, that political terrorism was abating. With the Moscow show trials any such promise evaporated. The execution of eight Soviet generals in June 1937 astonished more on account of the prominence of the victims than the methods invoked; the sinister routine of arrest by secret police, secret cross-examination, public confession and execution, had become sickeningly familiar, and Rees drew parallels between Stalin and Hitler in their determination to destroy any vestiges of political independence within their respective armies. Stalin governed as an Asiatic despot and the generals had come into conflict with him; 'in the USSR that in itself is cause for capital punishment.'

As a primer of Soviet Russia Rees recommended *The Revolution Betrayed*. Trotsky's brilliant analysis showed how increased Soviet wealth had created a new bourgeoisie of bureaucrats, technicians and privileged party workers requiring a state dictatorship to defend it. The Communist Party in Europe never had been a mass party of the proletariat in the sense understood by Marx; rather, it was a party for directing the masses, in the control of dedicated professionals with an absolute faith in the revolution and their own revolutionary morality. Events after the First World War in Russia might as well have been the work of criminals as of political revolutionaries, claimed Rees in September 1938: 'For one of the purposes of a revolutionary morality, such as Lenin tried to instil, is to create a standard of virtue which will impel men of the highest character to commit acts which by any other standard must be judged atrocious.' Lenin created such a party in Russia: it made the revolution and the Soviet Union. Yet an alliance with Stalin was imperative; as Churchill, the arch-anti-Bolshevist, declared, he would gladly turn to Satan if it might help in the defeat of Hitler.

'I hate that England should perhaps have to fight again', Rees wrote to Shiela Grant Duff, 'but I think it is necessary. It is terrible that such things should be necessary.' A nation must prepare for war psychologically and spiritually; one needed an ideal of freedom, of justice and democracy, 'a hope by which men can live and for which, if need be, they will die'. Young men could be expected to respond: witness the volunteers who had fought and fallen in Spain; deluded and betrayed they might have been, 'but anyone who understands them must concede that they were animated by that kind of idealism to which so many British leaders have appealed with only partial success' (24 June 1938). But if there was to be another war to save democracy, then democracy must be seen to be worth fighting for – and for too many thousands in Britain it was 'no more than a system which deprived them of every means to a good life'. (The appeal of democracy to the Germans had all along been blunted by the fact that in the leading democractic nations mass unemployment was a permanent and characteristic feature of the economic system.) Things had to change. 'Only states which at home pursue programmes of fundamental social reform . . . can hope to oppose the totalitarian States with a passion and courage equal to or greater than theirs' (25 March 1938). From his earliest days at the *Spectator*, Rees had pressed for a broad antigovernment consensus on primary social issues. He dwelt on the scourge of unemployment (1936 was the year of Jarrow), advocating – this in the conservative *Spectator* – state intervention in the economy to overcome it; and on a minimum wage he was unbending: 'to modern consciences a society which does not fulfil this condition is intolerable . . . It [a living wage] would be cheap at the price, and would be largely repaid in savings in sickness benefit and medical treatment' (23 April 1937). The presence of two million jobless constituted in 1939 an intolerable waste and an immense national danger; it was permanent mass unemployment, far more than the Treaty of Versailles, that brought about the death of the Weimar Republic, 'unhonoured, unsung, and unregretted by the millions of men and women to whom the hated "system" could give nothing more than a miserable and meaningless life on the dole' (10 February 1939).

Rees's leaders on national defence were the ones which most polarized readers. From the moment of the bombing of Spain he urged a wholesale reorganization of the country's defence system to match the *Luftwaffe*'s power. As late as March 1939 he was castigating the government's 'unconquerable distaste' for devising defences against air attack. In June of that year the country accepted conscription. Even so, Rees appealed for the sympathetic handling of conscientious objectors, for it was necessary to preserve a fundamental unity on questions of national defence. (He suggested large-scale schemes of agricultural improvement, instancing the benefical impact of the Quakers on a distressed area like Brynmawr.) Then, in spring 1939, Rees put all his preaching into practice when he volunteered for military service, enlisting in the Royal Artillery Territorial Army. His exposure to military habits formed the subject of his last pre-war editorial (18 August 1939), a typically forthright piece on the inadequacies of Territorial organization and leadership. The truth was that the officer corps was drawn from too narrow a social class; the reserve of talent in the ranks vastly outweighed the abilities of commisssioned officers, 'some of whom treated the army as an extension of public-school life'.

It is here impossible to do justice to the range of Rees's journalism of the 1930s. His leaders might be technical pieces on economics, though he was also regularly drawn to questions of broader social concern. Education is a case in point. A University Grants Committee report (1936) allowed him to take issue with the view that the university was a world in miniature where students enjoyed a general training in mind and body. Looking to Oxford and Cambridge, the committee recommended for the great civic non-residential universities more halls of residence, an extension of the tutorial system, and increased opportunities for physical training. This view, profoundly English, was (or so Rees considered) profoundly misguided: a university exists above all for the sake of advancing knowledge and for promoting in its students a capacity for vigorous and accurate thought. To these ends, the provision of halls of residence, refectories, gymnasia and unions must be subsidiary to the provision of libraries and a full complement of research and teaching staff. The world at large provided students with social experience; within the university, 'libraries are more important than swimming baths'. Rees saw secondary education in a similar light:

> The road home from school is in many senses a greater teacher than the school itself; and by far the greatest influence on a child's character and personality will come from his life outside the school, and especially his family. So far as the school tries to exercise that influence itself it is likely to diminish the efficiency with which it performs its proper function, which is, above all, that of imparting knowledge. (6 January 1939)

Knowledge was perhaps the greatest and most enduring of life's pleasures; 'that it should become one in childhood is the greatest service a system of education can give'. He had in mind his own intellectual awakening in Cardiff and doubtless his daily walk through the commercial hubbub of City Road; a little eastward lay the High School, fittingly approached via Oxford Lane.

Chapter III

From his time as an undergraduate London magnetized Rees; arriving there was like arriving in Paris or Berlin – the same exciting sensation of entering a great European cultural capital. His own personal magnetism served him well in literary-intellectual circles and captivated men and women who would dramatically impinge on his life. Yet if Rees was at ease in London, leading the bachelor life in Ebury Street, he never could imagine himself as anything but Welsh. In print and on the radio he expounded the differences between England and Wales: above all, how the political conservatism of the English, a natural disposition among the rich and successful, was something difficult for a Welshman to accept. Wales was by instinct 'progressive' (a favourite thirties word): 'we have wanted better conditions for the working man, greater equality and greater freedom and above all, more education. And this instinct and desire for social reform is shared by the large majority of our people.'[18] Faced with a difference so profound – and, questions of language apart, Rees maintained that a person from Wales would feel more at home in any other European capital rather than in London – the Welsh coped with being in England by banding together, largely in their chapels and societies.

Not every Welsh institution met with his approval. Some ossified the nation, feeding her sentimental illusions about her cultural and spiritual worth. 'How often in Wales have I not been told to be proud of my country, of its history, its heroes, its literature, religion and language?' he asked in 1934.[19] 'Why is it that, when I think of such things, they become mere phrases shouted at me by eloquent and pompous orators?' The real object of admiration should be the fighting instincts of the miners, which had made the south Wales coalfield a force in the modern world ('there is no comparable achievement in Welsh history'). Through organized unionism, the south Wales worker had affected the course of capitalism and the history of the working class. 'What is bombast in other Welshmen is the plain truth in the Welsh miners . . . Among them we can find our nationality.' Though Rees came to accept his propensity to romanticize the south Wales miners, he never ceased to regard them as the most advanced and dynamic element in the British labour movement. Hence his reaction to *The Road to Wigan Pier* (1937). Rees found much to admire in the book, but regretted that it could find no room politically for an active working class; it could not conceive of a socialism that was not essentially driven by those middle-class intellectuals whom Orwell had come to despise. He 'scarcely mentions a trade union or local Labour Party or Council except to deride them', although the Labour Party and the trade union movement were the two most solid achievements of the British working class. Wales had shown that the industrial workers could be an effective motor for socialism, so that the natural complement to Orwell's truthful description of the miners' working life was not his appeal to London intellectuals, but 'an account of the collier's struggle, as difficult and heroic as his life in the pit, to create the South Wales Miners' Federation'.[20]

Claims by literary Marxists of solidarity with the workers had their amusing aspects – not least to one another. According to Stephen Spender, at one public meeting Rees insisted 'that he had sprung from the working classes and would at this moment be a miner but for the extenuating circumstances (perhaps to be regretted after all!) of a scholarship to Oxford'.[21] Louis MacNeice described the same occasion: C. Day-Lewis spoke first,

in his tired Oxford accent, qualifying everything, nonplussed, questioning. Then Goronwy, who was just as Oxonian as Day-Lewis, took over and spoke like a revivalist, flashed his eyes, quivered with emotion, led with his Left and followed with his Left, punch on punch, dogma on dogma, over and over-statement, washed in the blood of – well, nobody asked of whom, but it certainly made you stop thinking.

Exhausted by the performance, Rees suggested oysters at Pruniers, the fashionable St James's restaurant. Others on the intellectual Left were teased as upper-middle-class public-school boys trumpeting the workers' cause. Rees's case is more problematic. Oxonian he might have appeared, but where did he really belong? 'Underbred', sniffed Virginia Woolf (she thought the same of Joyce and Lawrence), while A. L. Rowse hailed a fellow proletarian Celt – before deciding he'd been deceived: Rees was decidedly middle-class Welsh. Where *does* one place the son of a spiritual physician, elect of the righteous elect? Rees looked to his origins, to a farming background in Cardiganshire and a grandfather carting milk in Stepney. This was the Welsh way. The grammar-school sixth-formers at Cardiff might have been the sons of schoolteachers, bank officials, butchers and ministers, 'but our station in life, our cultural traditions, our social relationships were much closer to those of the working class . . .'[22] In any case, English class distinctions did not fit in Wales, where a more democratic spirit prevailed; the Welsh were a comparatively united people and one expression of this unity, so Rees repeated, was 'our common wish for social change and progress'.

A positive belief in socialism led Rees to make the case for Welsh home rule; a just nationalism furthered the unity of nations, because 'only when nations are able to do as they will with what is their own and no one else's will they be able or willing to join with each other in administrating what they have in common'.[23] He sought to counter the notion that Welsh nationalism was fanatical, resembling the nationalist movements of Italy and Germany. Nor did the delegation of powers from Westminster and Whitehall to a parliament in Wales strike him as impracticable, since there would be devices for reconciling this measure of self-determination with membership of a wider political and economic bloc. And he also dismissed the notion that Wales was too poor to afford self-government: 'If self-government implies complete isolation, no country is rich enough to afford it.' Yet this was not the pivot of his case.

The important question is what we Welshmen are to do with our country, our traditional way of life, and, not least, with ourselves. At present we can do little or nothing with these things because, ultimately, we are not responsible for them; and this fundamental irresponsibility has by now entered very deeply into the Welsh character.

Too many farcical institutions professed to safeguard Welsh culture ('the Eisteddfod flourishes more ridiculously than ever'), yet by some miracle a cultural tradition survived; even so, 'no culture is safe, or can prosper, which is divorced from political responsibility'. The point is a fundamental one, from which Rees never deviated. He had no difficulty with the idea of self-government; it was the Welsh nationalists of whom he despaired. In 1937 he had spoken admiringly of Saunders Lewis's services to Welsh literature; a year later he was treating Plaid Genedlaethol Cymru and its president with amused contempt: the nationalists had wandered into political fantasy in their admiration for Hitler (whom Lewis, at the time of Munich, saw as 'reasonable, and above all restrained and most suggestive . . . in new ideas').[24] Thereafter Rees would insist that Lewis was of the opinion that Hitler's victory in the war was acceptable if that meant the survival of the Welsh language.

Rees took more satisfaction in literary developments in Wales and applauded those English-language writers associated with Keidrych Rhys's new journal, *Wales*. Goronwy was among the group of sympathizers whom Keidrych approached in 1937 in the hope that they would lend support to a risky publishing venture. Rees was full of admiration for the enterprise, though privately he questioned whether it was appropriate for Keidrych to 'speak of ourselves as rooted in Wales when so much of the idiom in which *Wales* is written is that of contemporary English letters of the most fashionable and Bloomsbury kind. If, as you say, you really are of the People, you must write a language that the people can read.'[25] Publicly, he curbed his criticism, praising on the Welsh Home Service an excellent magazine whose contributors measured themselves by standards common to all the literatures of Europe. Adopting this perspective was crucial. Rees did not doubt Welsh artistic potential – 'my people seem to me to possess more of those qualities I admire, of passion, intelligence, individualism, and of natural devotion to culture than almost any other I have known'[26] (the Jews were his exception, a people he much admired and among whom he found many friends) – but the Welsh curse was provincial-mindedness, a refusal to submit to the international standards by which really exceptional talent is judged. The *Wales* stable of writers understood the truth of this.

Surprisingly, Rees himself reviewed almost no Anglo-Welsh literature for the *Spectator*, though he took the occasional batch of literary titles. He found few satisfactions in 'that vast and desolate Depressed area, the Land of Fiction'; the English novel was blighted by an untruthfulness, arising from the profoundly misguided assumption that people were particular and unique – and important because they were unique. From this flowed the novel's fixation with characters; with creations 'so particular, so specific that they exclude everyone and everything else but themselves'. It gave to English novels their claustrophobic, imprisoning quality. Truly great novelists had an acute awareness of the external world and were more concerned with men and women, not as psychological cases, but as social human beings, representative of forces that transcended the individual. It was a tragic view of life; it was also a Marxist view of life, and perhaps only one living writer had fully exploited it in fictional terms:

> M. Malraux sees men with all the infinite possibilities and variations of the classes, the interests, they represent, with the vitality of the forces which work through them, and, in addition, with the moral grandeur of men engaged in a conflict too vast to be exhausted in any clash of individuals. They are the agents of a doom and a destiny. (21 August 1936)

In common with other intellectuals in the 1930s, Rees looked to a type of continental writer and thinker, toughened in the political arena and desirous of social impact. The transgressive artist attracted him: men like Baudelaire, Balzac, Flaubert and Stendhal, who united a hatred for their society, its corruption, idiocy and hypocrisy, with an extraordinary talent for seeing it as it was. Plato was right: artists *are* dangerous people, and if genuinely alive and creative they must expect to be regarded as 'something between a leper and an anarchist'.

Rees delivered his opinions with vigour and wit. Nabokov left him cold: *Despair* was a joke and, once seen through, 'the shoddiness of its materials can no longer be concealed'. His comment, in a review of Mulk Raj Anand's *Two Leaves and a Bud* (30 April 1937), that the British system of indentured labour on Indian tea estates was one 'beside which the slave system which Lincoln fought a civil war to abolish was perhaps a paradise', led to protests which forced a partial climbdown – which in turn prompted Anand to defend him in the *Spectator* (11 June 1937): 'Mr Rees's estimate of their [the labourers'] position as "exploited, starving, cheated, dirty, diseased" still holds good to a degree unimagined by the complacent directors of the monopolies which control the tea industry.' Isolated judgements surprise, such as Rees's early approving estimate of John Betjeman as the religious poet of the lower middle classes, or his mauling of Auden and MacNeice's *Letters from Iceland* (1937). He greatly admired Auden the poet, but this book reduced its nominal subject to a backdrop – a squalid, primitive landscape redeemed only by glaciers, geysers and other 'sights'. It becomes an excuse for authorial introspection; and it is 'difficult not to see in Mr Auden's rigid obsession with himself, his friends, his acquaintances, an attempt . . . to reduce the world to a more manageable condition; it is in part a confession that the objective world is escaping him, is too much for his art' (3 September 1937).

Here Rees might have been speaking about his own past fiction. Even before *The Summer Flood* appeared, he was anxious for a new approach, one which moved outside the heads of his characters, 'turning all the doubts, conflicts and desires inside them into a real world of people and events'. The characters of modern fiction (he had *The Waves* in mind) had no vital social existence, and were really nothing but points of view: 'We never see them in their independent reality, freed from the excrescences, the fictions, the passions, with which they are clothed in the minds of others . . . '[27] This fresh challenge tested Rees to the limits. 'My new book promises well,' he wrote to Douglas Jay, 'but I can't get on with it, no satisfactory style, the old will not do and there is an embarrassment of a vague, unformed mass of material.' One half-finished novel abandoned (and seemingly torn to pieces), Rees completed the draft of another but with with no strong conviction of success. His fears proved justified. *A Bridge to Divide Them* (April 1937) moves ambitiously across the boundaries – Welsh mining valley to English estuary port, working-class squalor to middle-class comfort, domestic tribulations to public wheeler-dealing – yet in no particular setting does Rees seem fully at ease. He begins in Wales, with a restless, dissatisfied young collier whose social and psychological alienation foreshadows a violent end. An outsider with a streak of daring, Johnny is irresistible to women. But other torments afflict him, including (very briefly) religion – 'a good boy', explains the Methodist minister, 'though not very clear in the head'. Johnny abandons his pulpit-soapbox for lessons in economics and history at the home of a radical Nonconformist schoolmaster. 'Don't the men need leaders?' asks Mr Jones, 'clever men who can't be bought?' But Johnny settles for Annie, Mr Jones's singular housekeeper, with whom he decamps to Cardiff, thence to a port across the mouth of the Severn.

Rees is at his best on Welsh terrain, treating of adolescent yearning and treacherous small-town morality: the sexual itch and furtive release before the long confinement of marriage. With the move into England we are offered slow-motion pictures of upper-middle-class life as lived in the circle of Harcourt Best, a local magnate obsessed by his vision of a great steel bridge to span the estuary between two industrial towns. Some quiet fixing removes a major obstacle to the project, thereby dooming a plan for slum regeneration and leading, indirectly, to the pregnant Annie's death. Rees explores this alien universe largely through the turmoils of the young; English sophistication allows for some sharing of partners – whereas Johnny was beaten senseless for taking his butty's girl – but this kind of upper-class tolerance bespeaks a coldness of the heart. We see it through Rachel's eyes, in her stolen moments with Johnny, now a stoker on her Uncle Harcourt's ferry. Rachel's idealization of Johnny – the labourer worthy of his hire – breaks on the realities of his everyday life. And Johnny is angered by love (a precondition of capture in marriage) and prevented by a strain of nihilism from feeling part of anything outside himself. So he engineers his own and his enemies' death. Rachel is unmoved; he was a creature of her imaginings; little known in life, in death he becomes a stranger.

The novel articulates some of Rees's private concerns, not least the self-absorption that characterized his early years. Yet for most of its length *A Bridge to Divide Them* lacks authenticity; its message is loosely political – the cost of Best's ambition on the lives of those around him – but improbabilities of plotting heighten an already uncomfortable literariness. A proletarian novel, a study of bourgeois manners, a Lawrentian blending of the two (English rich girl falls for Welsh manual labourer), the novel disappointed most critics. Rees gave up on the genre, at least until after the war; he had no natural aptitude for plotting, for presenting convincing characters in plausible situations and relating them satisfactorily to a proper social environment. It would be some years before he recognized that he was his own best character, that his life had been more interesting and revealing than any fiction he could invent: at which point he found his *métier*, a literary fusion of autobiography and cultural analysis which would stand as the testament of a generation.

A Bridge to Divide Them carried the dedication 'To E.B.', a gesture famously met by the recipient, Elizabeth Bowen, with a slashing portrait in *The Death of the Heart* (1938) of a young man named Eddie, taken to be Goronwy. Bowen first met Rees at Oxford, within Maurice Bowra's gifted circle, and by 1936 they had begun an affair. Ten years his senior, the solidly married Bowen, versed in liaisons of this kind, seemed well armoured for the sexual battlefield – she reported that Rees had told her that though 'amiable I am heartless and see men as trees walking: perhaps in most cases I do'. Yet she could be wounded, and to judge by *The Death of the Heart*, Rees's desertion cut deep: for in September 1936, during a weekend house party at Bowen's Court in County Cork (Isaiah Berlin, Stuart Hampshire, John Summerson and Roger Senhouse were other guests) he abruptly transferred his affections to the beautiful Rosamond Lehmann. 'I suppose Eddie is Goronwy', wrote John Betjeman on reading the novel. The identification was natural. Eddie at twenty-three is 'the brilliant child of an obscure home' who knows his Bible by heart. Goronwy's fabled wrestlings over identity are present ('I suppose, that I'm I at all is just a romantic fallacy') and the resulting difficulties with women ('in the full sense you want me, I don't exist'). Eddie's explanation for taking Daphne's hand in the darkened cinema under the nose of Portia (a transmutation of the Bowen's Court betrayal and humiliation), has become much quoted: 'I have to get off with people . . . Because I cannot get on with them.' This might stand as a gloss on Rees's philandering (with intellectually able women particularly), but more disturbing in the Eddie/Goronwy parallel is the cruel social placing done by a writer alert to every nuance of class. Proletarian to the core, in physique, taste and morality, Eddie comes to Oxford defenceless (his family, 'from an obscure province', naturally carry no weight). A clever, entertaining freak, he gets by on charm and looks.

Having first welcomed the novel, Rees became aggrieved, seemingly to the point of threatening libel action. One understands his confusion. Eddie as a fictional character works exceedingly well and is clearly a composite creation drawn from more than one source. Nevertheless, as Diana Trilling has complained, considered as a representation of Rees, Bowen's portrait is grossly reductive.[28] Trilling makes two further points in relation to Rees's image as cad: that at this time he was free, or at least not anchored in marriage (unlike both Bowen and Lehmann), and that he, in contrast to the women, maintained a graceful silence on these private matters. Actually, the novel was not Bowen's last word on Rees. Her short story, 'A Walk in the Woods' (1941), has Carlotta, a suburban wife, escaping one Sunday for a trip outside London with Henry, her neighbour's lodger. He is ten years her junior, an age gap starkly apparent to some passing schoolgirls. 'They saw a haggard woman with dark red hair and a white face', a woman old enough to be his mother. Henry is fretful, lamenting the course of an affair that survives on clandestine meetings. 'It's my only life', Carlotta replies. 'You're my only life. My only way out. Before you came, I was walled in alive. I didn't know where to turn. I was burning myself out . . . ' But she knows the relationship is doomed; in the autumn dusk, as the trippers prepare for home, she sees Henry's life 'curve off from hers, like one railway line from another, curve off to an utterly different and far-off destination'.

Next on the literary front Rees turned to Georg Büchner (author of *Wozzeck*) and in collaboration with Stephen Spender prepared a translation of *Dantons Tod* (1835). This epic drama, pivoting on the clash between Danton and Robespierre amid the chaos of the French Revolution, spoke to the British Left, as it had done a decade previously to the German expressionist theatre. Büchner was fascinated by the 'terrible fatalism of history' – how events take up individuals who once might have seemed to be creating them. 'We haven't made the Revolution, the Revolution made us', as Danton puts it. Rees's introductory essay draws out the relevant strands: the masses as sole vehicles for social progress, the intertwining of the personal and political, and the inexorable momentum of the Revolution. For Rees, the tragedy of Danton is that after his great September days he is no longer an agent of history with a function to perform; the curse of the 'must' passes to Robespierre and Saint-Just. The notion of historical necessity captured Rees's generation. 'A great man is a man with a genius for history', he wrote in 1938; he might have added 'or woman', since only in La Pasionaria's presence had he felt a physical awareness of greatness. ('You are history. You are legend', she would comfort the departing International Brigades at Barcelona.)

It was the artist's relationship to the events of the time that occupied Rees in his last piece of writing before the army fully claimed him. In spring 1939 he took his fight against fascism beyond the *Spectator* offices by enlisting in the Territorials; six months later, he was mobilized as a gunner in the Royal Artillery. This volunteering for military service amazed his intellectual friends, whose position was best summed up by Cyril Connolly in *Horizon* (May 1940): 'War is the enemy of creative activity and writers and painters are right and wise to ignore it.' Two months later came Rees's reply.[29] This war was a just one, and on its outcome depended the continued activity of the artist; others may find ways of living under fascism but not the artist, for whom fascism has no room except as martyrs. Rees was not asking that all artists take up arms, or even commit themselves to any kind of political or social activity. But they should not avert their eyes. Artistic responsibility, 'while imposing no restraint on forms of expression or even the most ambiguous machinery of mythology, or fantasy or imagery [implied] that the content of the artist's imagination should be the reality of his time'. This responsibility would be discharged even if in the light of his understanding the artist could only, in the end, condemn or oppose the war. This, asserts Rees, was no more than a reiteration of the classical, fundamentally sane, relationship between the artist and the public, which both have an interest in maintaining.

> The complement of your advice that the artist should ignore the war is that the soldier, who must die that the artist may live, will find no voice which may speak for him what he wishes all the world to know, even more, no imagination that may illuminate for him the experience he knows but cannot comprehend . . . His enormous sacrifice will have no interest for those who alone are worthy and capable of communicating it; his expense of spirit and blood, his patience and endurance, his dim confused consciousness of their

significance, will speak and be spoken of only in the stale rhetoric of politicians and the falsehoods of war correspondents.

Connolly thought Rees's declaration sufficiently important to replace his own July 1940 editorial, and *Horizon* henceforth modified its stance of artistic indifference – by which time Rees was out of London, commissioned in the Royal Welch Fusiliers.

Chapter IV

To begin with, army life at RA headquarters in Bloomsbury proved monotonous and unstimulating. Rees saw friends in the evenings, or settled down to Isaiah Berlin's new book on Marx. By the turn of the year came hopes of a commission, a proper recognition of Rees's potential, thought the military historian Major-General Sir Ernest Swinton, a fellow of All Souls and one of his referees. 'You've got all the brains and guts and leadership necessary,' he reassured Goronwy, 'so do not give the impression of slackness and casualness!' Gunner Rees smartened up sufficiently for Sandhurst and on 23 March 1940, four months after his thirtieth birthday, became a second lieutenant in the Royal Welch Fusiliers. Embarked on training in military intelligence, he soon was giving classes himself; early on it fell to him to inculcate pride in the regiment by recounting its victories and defeats ('I feel like Homer', he wrote to Rosamond Lehmann). A little later at Cambridge he was instructing Freddie Ayer and Robin Zaehner on the interrogation of prisoners of war.

'So many vicissitudes and changes and journeys', Goronwy told his father – and the greatest still to come. In early summer 1940 Rees met the young Margaret (Margie) Morris, daughter of a Liverpool underwriter, in circumstances he recalled for a television interview with John Morgan in 1978:

> During the war I was stationed at Parkgate near Liverpool, and near our Mess was a house belonging to Margie's parents, and they were very kind to us and asked us over to play tennis and have drinks and that sort of thing. And there I got to know this girl. She was then nineteen and had only recently left school. She'd been driving a lorry during the Liverpool blitz and was then working on a lathe, and she was in every kind of way different, really, from any girl I'd ever known before, in the sense that she was entirely unacademic. All her

Rees and Margie on their wedding day. 'We all appreciated the strength and stability that she brought into his life, apart from her complementing his looks and charm' (A. J. Ayer).

gifts were practical gifts; in fact, they were all the gifts I don't have, and it somehow seemed the most natural thing in the world to marry her.

Friends saw it differently – for them it would be an act of the grossest irresponsibility for Rees to marry anyone – but, 'She makes me feel happier than I've ever expected to be', he had to confess to Rosamond,[30] and five days before Christmas 1940 he and Margie were married. His decision proved singularly fortunate: 'It turned out to be the happiest marriage one could possibly have had', said Rees, a verdict with which others agreed, attributing the success entirely to Margie. (Diana Trilling has remarked that in later years praise for Margie went hand in hand with condemnation of Rees, at least among the men; women readily confessed Goronwy's appeal: 'probably the most attractive man I have ever met', echoed Trilling.)

Rees's military career was by every account a successful one, the war revealing personal qualities as surprising to himself as to others. The unruly private soldier became a liaison officer under Montgomery and finished as a lieutenant-colonel with the occupying forces in Germany. By this time he was more diplomat than soldier, having joined the British Element of the Control Commission, an organization agreed by the Allies for the administration of Germany after her capitulation. In April 1945 he transferred to the commission's political division, settling down in Berlin to prepare regular reports on developments in the city and in the north-western British Zone where, at the level of province, military government detachments were being established. Rees's journalistic acumen and expert knowledge of Germany proved to be substantial assets: working alongside Rees, Noël Annan found him a perspicacious and amusing colleague whose desk was not for routine business ('although occasionally it might be disfigured by a small sheet of paper'). He relished Goronwy's account of the Allied victory parade of 7 September 1945. Marshal Zhukov was adamant that, as captors of Berlin, the Russians should lead the parade, and to ensure that no one took precedence he assembled his troops at four o'clock in the morning.

> The parade itself was impressive; but perhaps its most impressive feature was Marshal Zhukov himself who took the salute at the saluting base. In a Prussian-blue uniform, his burly chest blazing with decorations from his belt to his epaulettes, he threw the other commanders completely into the shade . . . The Russians had evidently seized the opportunity of the parade to give an impressive display of their military power. They threw in their heaviest armour, including Marshal Zhukov, and one wonders what impression it made on the eight visiting American congressmen, who in snap-brim hats, chewing gum, and smoking cigars looked as invincibly civilian as the Marshal looked warlike.[31]

A review of Stephen Spender's *European Witness* (*Spectator*, 1 November 1946) gave Rees the chance to convey some impressions of Germany in defeat – 'the great dead cities that lay at the end of every road, the jagged edges of shattered steeples pointing above the cornfields on every horizon, the endless vistas and avenues of devastation' – and his own immediate reactions to the annihilation of an evil:

> It was a masterpiece that could only have been achieved through complete control of technical and scientific method. To appreciate this masterpiece fully it was not enough merely to look at these ruins. One had to live among them, walk among them on a fine summer's day and savour the sweet smell of corpses, breathe the infected air heavy with the dust of acres of rubble, watch the rats growing fat and sleek among the debris and the baby in the garden growing quieter and yellower every day until its face had the smooth consistency of old wax.

And who was responsible for all of this? Rees would have said the Germans, who had lost a war they had deliberately planned and provoked. Spender's culprits were the Nazis, the demonic German leaders by whom the people were possessed. Rees thought highly of *European Witness* – apart from its treatment of Nazism. Spender's Nazis were literary creations, out of Goebbels, Hitler, Dostoevsky and Ernst Jünger; he could offer no flesh-and-blood adherents, even though they peopled the country in their millions. For the Nazi is neither demonic nor diabolic:

> He is short and fat, carries a leather despatch case and even among the ruins he presses his trousers every night. He is a human being who is entirely at the mercy of social and economic conditions; and one is inclined to think that whenever and wherever these conditions degenerate below a certain level he turns and rends himself in panic. He is far more frightening than Mr Spender's demons; moreover, he exists.

Rees's realism on post-war Germany impressed a Cambridge audience in August 1946. He spoke on the German problem, which, simply stated, was how to eliminate the elements of danger, and yet preserve the benefits which a reconstructed

Germany could confer on Europe.[32] He rejected the Morgenthau plan for reducing Germany to an agricultural community and dismissed proposals for dismembering the country into a number of separate states. Germany had to survive as a complete economic unit, for only by the fullest employment of its productive capacity could it make its proper contribution to European recovery. Furthermore, only in a productive Germany could the political goals of the Atlantic powers be met. The Germans had to see for themselves that democracy was not a set of abstract principles but a practical system of government. It was the political face of a social revolution and never could be created on the foundation of economic decay. This was the folly being committed by the Allied government: 'The spectacle of well-fed administrators attempting to teach democracy to an audience of the starving and undernourished is one of nauseating hypocrisy and futility and the attempt can only end in discrediting democracy itself.' The solution to the German problem was one which allowed her to stand economically on her own two feet. Security was a broader issue; a system for guaranteeing security against Germany alone would only increase the level of general insecurity, whereas a system strong enough to contain the great powers would be effective in restraining Germany. 'You cannot make peace as if you were still making war', concluded Rees arrestingly.

If Rees's subject matter was predictable, his Cambridge audience was certainly not, for he had chosen to address a Liberal Party summer school. Even more surprising had been his decision, in January 1945, to allow his name to go forward as the prospective Liberal candidate for Caernarfon: local activists could be assured of his radicalism – if not of his party membership. Though he failed to make the shortlist, Caernarfon got its Goronwy: the young Goronwy Roberts won the seat for Labour (his victory in Lloyd George's old constituency coming to symbolize the eclipse of Liberalism in Wales). Far more interested in political culture than in narrow party politics, Rees could not seriously have contemplated a parliamentary career, and his choice of the Liberals is quizzical, to say the least: an act of filial piety perhaps, or a response to overtures from Welsh Liberals desperate for a bright new face. At Cambridge the Liberal leader Clement Davies, who held R. J. Rees in the greatest affection, greeted Goronwy like a long-lost son. (Though the Liberal attachment waned, Rees found himself – 'to my horror' – speaking in 1950 on behalf of the Liberal candidate at Finchley – a neighbourly gesture which did not prevent him voting Labour in 1951.)

By 1946 Rees had embarked on a wholly new career, having spent a mere three months (following his demobilization) working again on the *Spectator*. He gave as his reason for quitting an inability to face what he imagined lay before him, the task of writing endlessly about the cold war. His sentiments are understandable – and if ever a time seemed right for new beginnings it was the end of the war – yet one has to regret the abandonment of intellectual journalism; it was a world that suited him well, and to which he returned with distinction for the last fourteen years of his life. Withdrawal from the *Spectator* produced yet another remarkable about-turn, this one directing Rees into commercial life. Before the war he had become exceedingly friendly with the novelist Henry Green, a man of democratic tastes, notwithstanding his Eton and Oxford background. He loved pubs and football, gossiping and flirting, and, again like Rees, he read voraciously across the range of fiction. Green's real name was Henry Yorke and he made his living by managing Henry Pontifex Ltd, the family firm of engineers, brass founders and coppersmiths. At Henry's invitation Rees became a co-director, remaining in the business for seven prosperous years. 'Most people', Richard Wilberforce insists, 'underestimated Goronwy's practical ability . . . I had many talks with him about machine tools & production & sales – he enjoyed that world and made something positive out of it.' As it happened, Rees had other employment: afternoons found him slipping away from Pontifex to the offices of MI6, where he served in political intelligence at the Russian and German desks.

The Pontifex years produced a full-length novel, his first in a dozen years, helped by daily lunch breaks set aside for writing. Published by Chatto & Windus in June 1950, *Where No Wounds Were* took its title from a line in 'Strange Meeting', Wilfred Owen's poem of the First World War, in which an English officer in a dream identifies himself with the enemy he has killed. In Rees's dreamlike novel a captured *Luftwaffe* pilot comes to request enlistment in the RAF. Adam Lipansky has landed his aircraft intact in England. Why? The answer is something which a British intelligence officer, working in a strange decaying mansion vaguely located in London, has to root out. Free of all physical intimidation, the interrogation becomes an exploration of Nazi ideology and the German cast of mind. Two systems of belief are opposed. The young, arrogant Lipansky faces a world-weary army captain whose shabby turnout and passive amateurism suggest a world destined for oblivion. Through Lipansky's introspective musings and flashbacks into his past, Rees builds up a vivid picture of the making of a National Socialist. Here he is on firmest ground, alive to the shifting elements of German militarism: the Prussian officer code stressing honour, decency and courage; and the new barbarianism, a political technique and ideology founded on unlimited fear.

'Nazi Germany was precisely thus', said James Hanley, reviewing the novel; and yet more chilling is its account of National Socialism's popular appeal. For the masses are the basis of the movement; the people crave a sense of community, under a purposeful leader who will give them bread and work. They are sick to death of weak-willed democracy and its cosmopolitan cultural absurdities. 'We know what we are doing,' Lipansky tells his interrogator, '. . . we like this world. We feel at home in it . . . whatever happens in this war, your day is over.' Germany represents the future, against the old duplicities of crumbling liberal democracy. Totalitarianism must triumph, especially in a ruined Europe where millions will be reduced to extremes of poverty and misery. 'Do you imagine for a moment that people in those conditions will listen to your pitiful catchwords about liberty, equality, fraternity? You might as well talk to rats in a sewer about democracy as to the people of Europe after this war is over.' But how convincing is this eloquence, even to the speaker? Is it not empty rhetoric booming in a spiritual void? Lipansky from the beginning harbours obscure self-doubts. Crucially, he is kept apart from other prisoners, and solitary contemplation in the man of action raises fears and questionings: kept in isolation, the prisoner begins to interrogate himself. An inner voice now chimes with the interrogator's ('patient, inexorable, never ceasing – sometimes it seemed to be his own'), and the British officer, once an object of scorn, becomes a psychologist, a father-confessor, Lipansky's conscience, even.

The novel's phase of outward dramatic action centres around Lipansky's successful escape. He stumbles across a London ablaze under aerial attack. The German bombardment elates him:

> He was overcome by a feeling of gaiety, almost frivolity, at the thought of so much history being brought to an end. The culture had seemed so rich, so solid, so permanent, that even the truest believers had not quite been able to imagine its final collapse. That had been a mirage that shone before them, a goal to be worked for, a purpose to be achieved and demanding infinite patience and self-sacrifice. Now that the moment of fulfilment had come even the believers would hardly credit it. And he, Lipansky, had been a witness of this moment.
>
> He could have danced for joy as he walked steadily and soberly on. He felt as if from now on life would be a fairy tale in which nothing would quite be as before. A great weight had been lifted from the shoulders of the world, which now would regain its first innocence. (p. 207)

This passage crystallizes Nazi nihilism and its ache for release from the burden of the past – which is the key to a vigorous life and decisive action for the future. 'The trouble is that, in some distorted way, you are all fanatical idealists', the interrogation officer challenges Lipansky; 'every mad airman has a volume of

Nietzsche in his knapsack.' Their dream is of a timeless Home, an ancient pastoral world of innocence and simplicity:

> If you walked through the fields at evening in the summer you came to a farm built in a square round the farmyard and on the farmhouse steps sat the heavy slow-spoken farmer who smoked his pipe, beside him his wife bent over her sewing and on the steps at their feet played the dreamlike children with their piercing blue eyes and bleach-white hair. In the barn that made one wing of the farmhouse the cows and oxen munched their fodder and stared out into the evening with the same untroubled eyes as their masters, over the farmyard hung the warm smell of their manure and away across the fields rose the dust of the deeply rutted lanes. (pp. 22–3)

Not even defeat on the battlefield had broken the assurance of these people; their virtues were the elemental ones, the soil the source of their strength. Then into their midst came 'the Chosen One', a leader who would expunge the national shame of the war and 'who promised to satisfy their deepest instincts, for farm and family and home . . . Among these farmers He found his first, and his last, disciples.'

In his escape Lipansky discovers another pastoral haven, inhabited by no race of heroes but by those willing to accept him, 'not for use, but for friendliness, companionship, affection perhaps'. He has reached the bald Welsh hills, another spiritual location, enshrining a Christian ideal of the equality of all men:

> Even the air had a quality that was pure and ancient. This country was so old that it had never lost its youth. The bare fields were shining and golden. They lay so far in the west that every evening for centuries the setting sun had spilled its radiance on them and had coloured even the air above. (p. 242)

In the stone-flagged living room of Tŷ Gwyn a tableau presents itself, a scene embedded in Rees's imagination from images of parents and grandparents in their own family homes:

The door opened on to a large low-ceilinged room that was revealed like a stage scene when the curtain rises. Only it seemed more like a painted interior, in which for centuries no detail had been changed, than a stage on which human beings live and move and act . . . In the wall on Lipansky's right was a huge darkened recess in which burned an open fire whose glow fell on the faces of two people, a man and a woman, who sat facing each other on the hearth. (p. 231)

Life in that room endures, as in Iago Prytherch's impregnable fortress, indifferent to the events and circumstances that have spawned a Lipansky:

It seemed an affront to everything he believed in that this house and its owners should have persisted through the years that had made him what he was. He had a moment of horrible perception that, like some primitive organism, they would still persist when all the violence in which he was a part should have spent itself. At that moment he realized that he no longer knew or valued what until then he had been fighting for all his life. He would fight no more. (p. 233)

Drawing on Rees's experience of interrogating one particular prisoner, *Where No Wounds Were* remains a readable novel of ideas with a powerful psychological dimension. Its excitements largely stem from the mental battle fought between intimate enemies and, more deeply, within one man's mind which is also the mind of a nation. (Hitler and Goebbels, Rees remarked, had done more damage to their countrymen than the entire RAF.) For more than one reviewer the politico-moral inquisition recalled *Darkness at Noon*, a telling comparison since Koestler's historical novel is both a political document and a psychological thriller. Rubashov's antagonist, like Lipansky's, is in part his alter ego, a presence who voices the questions the prisoner is asking of himself. For George Painter (Proust's biographer) the inward nature of the drama suggested Kafka's influence: Lipansky was not only a Nazi but Everyman – 'a fugitive from reason and individual freedom' – whose interrogator is his conscience; 'together they make up one being, and that being is ourselves'. Kafka was another of Rees's favourites, to whom he

A hallmark Chatto wrapper for Rees's 1950 novel, the story of a war within a war and a deep analysis of the Nazi mind.

next would turn by way of a translation of Gustav Janouch's *Gesprache mit Kafka* (*Conversations with Kafka*), published in German in 1951.

Before this, however, Rees's life would take further unexpected directions. At the end of 1950 the family moved from St John's Wood to Sonning-on-Thames, midway between London and Oxford, and thus the perfect location when, in April 1951, he became non-resident estates bursar of All Souls (the preferred choice of Geoffrey Faber, who had occupied the post since 1923). Not everyone judged Goronwy – a man known to live above his means – as the ideal custodian of college finances, but military responsibilities and the experience of Pontifex had sharpened his practical sense so that even A. L. Rowse, who violently opposed the appointment, had to concede that Rees proved a competent administrator. Richard Wilberforce, later estates bursar himself, goes further, judging Rees 'a *good* bursar – businesslike and quite imaginative. The farm tenants, of course, liked him a lot' (college estates ran to more than 3,000 acres in various parts of the country). Touring these estates, busying himself in committee, entertaining honorary graduands (Dean Acheson, Rab Butler, Somerset Maugham), Rees delighted in a job that allowed him to continue at Pontifex. His old friend Maurice Bowra became Oxford's new vice-chancellor and in March 1952 another good friend, John Sparrow, was elected warden at All Souls, despite his show of indifference ('two Sparrows don't make a Sumner', he commented at the time – a reference to Humphrey Sumner, the warden who had appointed Goronwy). Sparrow, so the story went, picked up a number of votes designed to keep out Rowse (then sub-warden), and Rees had been instrumental in organizing Sparrow's campaign.

Chapter V

INTERVIEWED IN THE *SCOTSMAN* IN DECEMBER 1972, REES SPOKE OF HIS life as a restless one, with 'far too many jobs taken on, too many worlds either conquered or left in a mild state of chaos because of [my] arrival on the scene'. His greatest mistake was to have accepted appointment as principal of University College, Aberystwyth, a verdict with which no one could disagree: it was an unfortunate move, for himself and for the college. The post had lain vacant for more than a year while Thomas Jones, the college's octogenarian president, having dismissed all internal applicants, sounded out likely candidates in Oxford, Cambridge and London. Rees's name came forward in May 1953, backed by Sparrow and Bowra; he had intellectual distinction, an administrative background, and was only partly deficient in a further requirement of the job, that the candidate be fluent in Welsh (Rees, who had grown up bilingually, promised to recover his spoken Welsh). Nevertheless, Tom Jones from the beginning anticipated opposition to Rees's appointment from nationalists within the college, and sure enough, primed by Sir David Hughes Parry (Jones's elected successor as president), they mounted an extravagant attack at a college council meeting in June. There Rees answered questions 'with dignity and lucidity and humour' (Tom Jones's words) and in so doing won the overwhelming backing of council members. The president felt relief and pleasure; the new principal and his wife were, 'a beautiful young pair, in the prime of their powers, facing their new adventure' (letter to Violet Markham, 4 August 1953).

Nationalists excepted, the appointment was widely welcomed in Wales; 'Mr Rees complies with all the conditions, explicit and implicit', deemed the *Western Mail*. To those who knew him better it was more a question of temperament. Could he possibly stand the job? Wouldn't he be a total misfit removed from the Oxford–London axis, his true social and intellectual province? 'On paper, it seemed an ideal set-up', Rees told the *Scotsman*. 'I had been born in the place, I'm a Welshman, I've moved in academic circles.' One might accept his further explanation, that he wished to commit himself more fully, both professionally and in the cause of Wales – as one must also acknowledge the material benefits attached to such a prestigious post, including a principal's salary (the Reeses' lavish lifestyle generally left them stretched) and a commodious house for four young children born between 1942 and 1948. Aberystwyth was alive for Rees largely as the landscape of youth, and his decision to return there was surely bound up with his own memories of childhood and home; he spoke of the kind of security enjoyed by children who grow up in places which once belonged to their fathers. (The appointment naturally delighted R. J. Rees, a long-time friend of Thomas Jones.) But whatever the emotional bonds, Goronwy had not lived in Wales since his school days, when Aberystwyth had been simply a place, and not the people who lived there. Now, as he prepared a radio talk on his feelings on returning to Wales, some lines from Gerard Manley Hopkins played in his mind: 'Lovely the woods, waters, meadows, combes, vales, / All the air things wear that build this world of Wales.' He tried, unsuccessfully, to suppress the next line – 'Only the inmate does not correspond.'

Rees's broadcast (28 September 1953) spoke of curiosity mixed with apprehension: curiosity about the degree to which he and his country might each have changed in the intervening years, and apprehension because he realized that in his part of Wales 'certain standards of conduct and belief commanded, in public at least, almost universal assent'.[33] He recalled the sense of liberation he felt when as a young man he had moved away to Oxford, to a place where he might express himself without fear of certain disapproval. Was he not 'voluntarily returning to the land of bondage'? First impressions were not reassuring. What struck him at Aberystwyth was the intense cultural and intellectual conservatism of the Welsh, a condition far removed from the dynamism of the nineteenth century, when Wales had created new institutions to meet her own particular needs. By contrast, he now perceived 'an inability either to create new institutions or to adapt existing institutions to the changed conditions of the present time'. Other western nations had experienced difficulties in coming to terms with revolutionary change, but for Wales the problem was intensified by the condition of her language. Welsh culture survived through the language, which must be protected and propagated ('if it dies, the people perish'), yet the language required an immense creative effort devoted to its development. Its present inadequacies helped explain why in many fields Wales seemed to be backward looking, living on an intellectual heritage fast dwindling under modern conditions. This was reflected, so Rees concluded,

> sometimes in an obsession with problems that have long since ceased to be real problems: sterile opposition to changes which are inevitable; sometimes in a passive acceptance of such changes without any effort to adapt them to local and national conditions. To a native returning, Wales seems to lie like a ship becalmed, waiting for some fresh breeze which will bring it once more under full sail.

The boldness of his Monday broadcast won a *Western Mail* editorial and ensured that on the following Saturday a thousand excited students would crowd the King's Hall on the sea front for the principal's inaugural lecture. He did not disappoint. Trumpets, bells and whistles gave way to attentive silence as Rees outlined his idea of a university.[34] He rejected the utilitarian argument – that universities should provide in the right quantities and proportions the specialists required by the state – as he did the notion of universities as factories of research. Instead, he took direction from Mark Pattison's life of Isaac Casaubon, and its observation that 'the scholar is greater than his books': that 'knowledge is not the thing known, but the mental habit which knows'. The successful student acquired such a mental habit through a direct exposure to those who pursued disinterested truth; through a personal understanding of 'that extraordinary game of question and answer which we call knowledge'. The universities were not the most effective institutions for the mass production of the nation's specialists, but one might hope that university students, if properly trained, would be equipped for becoming better specialists – and better people.

> They will be better because learning has its own virtues, of disinterestedness, of objectivity, of humility, and of integrity . . . the virtues of which the world stands in the greatest need today. It is precisely insofar as the universities have no utilitarian purpose, that they are the most useful of all institutions.

The students went away exhilarated. 'Here is a man one would like to work with', they enthused, and the co-operation bore immediate fruit as their run-down Union House was at last refurbished. Through all his Aberystwyth vicissitudes Rees never lost the regard and affection of the students, the bulk of whom were south Walians – 'completely unpretentious, pleasantly irreverent and egalitarian, and very quick to spot fraud or showmanship', in the opinion of Richard Cobb, at that time a recently appointed lecturer in history. The new principal did not treat them as children. He understood the mood of the 1950s: youthful in age and manner, he possessed (as the students' magazine put it) an 'informality without loss of dignity' that gave him 'a power . . . that mailed-fist tactics have conspicuously failed to achieve'. In a claustrophobic and hierarchical institution, he brought a style and glamour associated with the larger world. Student profiles dwelt on his 'versatility of achievement and cosmopolitan range' – something he quickly demonstrated with *Conversations with Kafka* (his translation of Gustav Janouch, published in 1953) and *The Answers of Ernst von Salomon* (1954), with its masterly foreword by Rees (Salomon's writings were honoured documents in the eyes of the Third Reich). In the summer of 1954 Rees travelled once more through Germany, gathering material for four BBC talks which afterwards appeared in the *Listener* (October 1954).

*Before the fall: Rees (third from the left) and Margie (second from the right)
at the Aberystwyth Old Students' Association dinner, 1954.*

For the two or more years at Aberystwyth that were relatively
trouble free, Rees remained productive extramurally. He returned to radio as the compiler of a programme on David Jones
and took part in a tribute to Dylan Thomas broadcast shortly
after the poet's death. He had known Thomas in London –
indeed, he had been likened to him: meticulous in his writing,
cavalier in his approach to life – and on becoming principal had
even suggested that the University of Wales award Thomas an
honorary degree (a prospect which delighted Dylan). Additionally, there was a radio adaptation of *Where No Wounds Were*,
produced by his old drinking companion, Louis MacNeice, one
of a number of notables brought to Aberystwyth by Rees. He
persuaded Isaiah Berlin to address the 1954 conference of
extramural tutors, an occasion launched by the principal with a
free-ranging lecture on the modern predicament.[35] As Rees saw
it, this was that 'state of pain, negation, and self-destruction' of

which Nietzsche was the prophet: 'I describe what is to come, what cannot now fail to come: the advent of nihilism.' Behind even those who had given rise to the notion of the nineteenth century as stable, confident and progressive was to be detected a malaise, a sense of uneasiness. It is revealed in their private lives as much as in their public gestures: 'the desperate unhappiness and frustration which underlay the public prosperity of so typical a Victorian as Browning; the extraordinary half-world of fantasy, despair and sheer hysteria and panic from which Ruskin's hysterical appeals to social morality emerged'. Rees considered the Nietzschean impulse in National Socialism, one of the two great heresies of the time. Communism, in theory at least, appealed to a sense of the individual's dignity and value (so affronted by National Socialism) and that millions accepted the chasm between communist principle and practice should, Rees suggested, surprise no one brought up as a Christian. The West's catastrophe was that the Soviet Union had captured its own ideas of human dignity and equality, of faith in human reason and confidence in the human spirit; 'indeed, in the unceasing intellectual war which the West is now waging against Communism it is very often its own discarded ideals which it is attacking'.

The long vacation of 1954 was a busy time for Rees. He accepted a Home Office invitation to serve on a committee examining the law relating to homosexuality and prostitution. Its chairman, John Wolfenden, had hesitated before taking up the appointment, fearing that such an assigment might damage the reputation of Reading University, of which he was vice-chancellor. Rees joined with no such qualms. The thirteen members were thought be open-minded and the committee's composition was intended to be representative of the nation at large (Rees's Welshness was a factor in his appointment). Of course, he had homosexual friends, and Patrick Higgins's study of Wolfenden suggests that these contacts were significant:[36] it was Rees who arranged for three powerful homosexual advocates to appear before the committee and throughout his time on

Wolfenden he proved an effective spokesman for change. That homosexual activity in private should be decriminalized was the general view of the committee, with Rees among the small majority arguing for eighteen as the age of consent. (Its final recommendation of twenty-one – urged by the chairman with the welfare of national servicemen in mind – actually became law in 1967 with the passing of the Sexual Offences Act.)

Away from Wolfenden, yet another radio commission opened up a new phase in Rees's writing: he contributed to a BBC series in which six people (C. P. Snow and Stanley Spencer among them) spoke of their early childhood. Goronwy alerted his father to what was to be an outstanding script on growing up as a child of the manse. The talk set him working on further autobiographical pieces, one on his undergraduate vacation in Silesia (*Encounter*, April 1956) and another revolving around Guy Burgess, a companion of the thirties and forties who, together with Donald Maclean, had mysteriously disappeared in 1951. 'Burgess was my oldest friend', Rees wrote to Chatto & Windus in November 1955, 'and one way and another I think I know more about him than anyone else . . . I feel I have to write it down, and am doing so at great speed, and very soon will send you some of what I have written.' Five months later his Burgess story appeared, in a form he could scarcely have imagined and under circumstances he must have dreaded.

Rees's entanglement with the Cambridge spy ring, the subject over decades of much fanciful speculation, has recently been elucidated: from research among the KGB archives we know that for little over a year (1938–9), and entirely in the anti-fascist cause, he co-operated in Burgess's Comintern activities by supplying political hearsay gathered from weekends at All Souls. With the Soviet–German non-aggression pact of August 1939 – when the Comintern switched from an anti-Nazi to an anti-western line – a thoroughly disillusioned Rees gave up on this activity. At the same time he promised not to reveal that Burgess (and Anthony Blunt) had been recruited as agents, on the understanding that they too had broken at this point. Yet

Rees's knowledge was potentially explosive, and Burgess was worried that it might slip out. This is why, in July 1943, when the Cambridge conspirators were at last operating productively, he advanced the extraordinary suggestion that Rees be physically liquidated – as the man who had enlisted Rees, he offered to do the job himself. As it happened, Rees kept his secret until after Burgess had defected, at which point he spoke to MI5. When in February 1956 the spies re-emerged in Moscow something more than a quiet word with British security was deemed appropriate. This said, why ever Rees should have allowed his Burgess material to appear in the form it did, butchered and sensational-ized for the Sunday tabloid press, still remains a mystery. Five flimsily anonymous articles published in the *People* (March–April 1956) became his death warrant, or 'a trigger to fire the rifle of intrigue right in his face', as the Aberystwyth student president put it.

The students might have adored him and the younger academics regarded him as largely on their side, but to some influential senior professors Rees was the metropolitan playboy (his white socks have passed into legend), the unconformable intruder, beyond assimilation. He found the nationalists his sternest opponents; their assumption of a superior patriotism dismayed him and he clashed with them philosophically on the question of a university's role in nation building. Rees rejected the idea of the university as a means of propagating a distinct-ively national culture, insisting that 'one of its functions must also be to produce people who will look at their own society from the outside and in relation to other societies and who will have a detached and critical view of their own society. Unless it gives them that it achieves nothing.'[37] As he saw it, learning at Aberystwyth was being made to come second to preserving Welsh culture. Rees's Wales, one has to repeat, was largely an amalgam of landscape, family and childhood ('in these we find a sense of actuality, because they have made us what we are'). He was comfortable enough in his Welshness but Welsh intellectual culture did not excite him and rarely could he place Welsh issues at the centre of his interests. It was inconceivable that it might be otherwise: 'I think it is terrible this feeling that the most important thing about you is being a Welshman.'

Rees's perceived anti-Welshness, rather than any rumpus over spies, is thought to have sealed his fate at Aberystwyth. He appeared to have ridden the storm surrounding the Burgess articles, despite the strategems of Sir David Hughes Parry and the professorial core whose wish to remove him from office was never a secret. Then some high-profile resignations from the college council swung events against him, more especially that of Sir Ifan ab Owen Edwards (son of Sir Owen M. Edwards and brother-in-law of Sir David Hughes Parry), who resigned in protest at the college's decision not to appoint a commission of inquiry into the principal's conduct. The professors now made their move and the Willink committee was duly constituted. For the remainder of the year (August–December 1956) a sidelined Rees, the object of feverish rumour and gossip, awaited its verdict. At least student support held firm, and to the very end: the principal, they insisted at an emergency general meeting (reported in the students' newspaper, *The Courier*, 22 June 1956), 'had increased the prestige of the College throughout the country. He had increased the material amenities of the students and had proved a fine leader; he had fostered progressive ideas; his interests were wide and sympathetic. Nothing could be further from the truth than to say that he was unfitted to be a leader of students . . . [it was] an honour and a privilege for students to defend him'. The Willink report judged otherwise. It arrived in February 1957, 'a vicious little mouse', thought Rees, believing that it savaged him on matters not central to his principalship. Having found no reason to question his 'financial probity, temperance, or sexual morality', nor his competence as a university administrator – 'The net effect of what we have read and heard leaves us with the impression of an academic community that was running well and smoothly' – the case against him rested on the publication of the *People* articles and his behaviour afterwards. On these matters the report was unsparing: 'In negotiating a remunerative contract with the *People*, the Principal offered material that was lewd and scandalous' (part of which, as he acknowledged, was 'exaggerated and unfair'), and in doing so he had shown 'a wanton disregard for the interests of the College'. Subsequently, 'having on the 10 April made an agreement with the President [to resign], he went back on his word'; his moves to remain in office, and in particular to avoid any committee of inquiry, were 'discreditable, and his attitude to the President of the College not only discourteous and offensive, but also unfair'.

On the motivation behind the Burgess articles, the report very largely accepted the Oxford viewpoint, that they were by way of a pre-emptive strike; that the reappearance of the spies in Moscow had provoked a panicky move designed to discredit any stories of past connections that Burgess might care to reveal. Rees's actions, repeated Willink, were 'self-regarding'; there was 'not from first to last any hint or suggestion that he gave a thought to the effect upon the College'. Rees's own explanation laid stress on the threat to national security still posed by Burgess. He had not operated alone, and his re-emergence in Moscow was a warning to fellow conspirators that they might be exposed if they did not continue in their work. 'What, of course, he [Rees] was out to do', reflected Noël Annan,

> was to expose Blunt and – let the chips fall where they might – name numbers of those who were friends of the spies and might, or might not, also be hidden agents. He suffered obloquy and social ostracism for his pains and his career was blasted while Blunt sailed serenely on.[38]

Here one should make plain that Rees's anti-communism was utterly genuine. He was almost as early an anti-communist as he was an anti-fascist. Reports out of Moscow in the post-war years, especially of the Soviet labour camps, confirmed how far was the revolutionary dream from the brutish communist reality – 'a degradation so absolute that not only the body but the spirit must submit', Rees had written; it was his opinion that anyone who remained in the Communist Party after the 1948 Soviet putsch in Prague hardly qualified as a human being. In a *Spectator* review of that year he violently turned on Marx, wondering how so repulsive a figure – 'overbearing, suspicious, arrogant, treacherous, Jesuitical, inspired by hate . . . incapable of truth or of loyalty, an egotist to the point of megalomania' – and with doctrines so at odds with reality, could ever have inspired the devotion of millions.[39] Noël Annan was correct in surmising that for Rees the eventual unmasking of Blunt vindicated his decision to publish what in 1956 was dismissed as hysterical nonsense. Rees's call for a public inquiry would likewise appear to have been justified, though it is doubtful whether such an inquiry would have dislodged the Establishment élite responsible for the government's security arrangements; as Annan memorably put it, 'The explosion detonated by these articles was atomic; but the blast-walls of the Establishment are so cunningly constructed that the person who was most hideously wounded was Mr Rees himself.'[40]

Rees's departure from Aberystwyth in April 1957 signalled the start of a bewildering downward spiral. Once (in his brother's words) 'the favourite of fortune, the golden boy for whom success followed success', he had brought disaster upon himself. Deserted by former friends, his career and reputation in ruins, he turned to Derek Verschoyle, a beguiling chancer known from *Spectator* days. Verschoyle, who in the post-war years had founded, then sold, a moderately successful publishing business, now persuaded Rees to join him in an ill-fated building venture based at Westcliff-on-Sea. But worse, in May 1957 Rees suffered a freakish motor accident at a garage near Maidenhead. His injuries were severe, requiring a massive blood transfusion and thirty-five stitches to the face. The scars healed beautifully, helped by some gentle sunbathing on a hospital verandah at Ascot, but his shattered left leg proved more stubborn and for the rest of his life Rees carried a slight limp.

With a large family to support (a fifth child had been born at Aberystwyth), he sought new avenues of income. Possible openings in television were discussed and some *Brains Trust* appearances negotiated. He sounded Denis Hamilton about assignments for the *Sunday Times* and accepted J. R. Ackerley's offer of a stint of fiction reviewing for the *Listener*. The BBC commissioned a translation from the German, while from Chatto & Windus came a contract for a volume of autobiographical sketches in the style of his *Encounter* pieces. Resettled more comfortably in Highgate, Rees set about his *Listener* reviewing, submitting in July 1958 the first of his fortnightly notices of novels of the day. He admired Joe Ackerley's scrupulous standards and was anxious not to disappoint him. Rees's tastes had changed little over the years. He lamented the tendency of novels (American ones in particular) to burden themselves with a dead weight of incident and description ('one sometimes feels surprised that such novels do not begin by explaining the principles of the circulation of the blood'). Doris Lessing was much more to his liking because she saw her characters in relation to complex social forces; it gave to their actions a significance wider than themselves. But there were other qualities in fiction, most of all an intensity of vision and imagination which allows the creation of worlds completely strange yet completely real (here Rees applauded Muriel Spark's *Memento Mori* and Iris Murdoch's *The Bell*). In Robbe-Grillet, intensity of vision becomes the claustrophobia of obsession; like others in France, he propounded a view of the novel which denies all possibility of generalization. 'All theories of fiction are wrongheaded and this more wrongheaded than most'; though in the case of *The Voyeur* Rees confessed a brilliant result: the mad attention to detail gave the novel 'a kind of optical realism which makes an uncanny effect'. Rees's responses were perceptive and personal and always crisply expressed. He welcomed Elizabeth Taylor who, like other women novelists, tends to persuade us that women have always had the worst and men the best of things – 'It looks so different from the other side!' he exclaimed. Colette wrote with an age-old feminine wisdom combined with the eye of a child or an animal: 'she writes as cats might write, which fortunately they can't.' Alexander Cordell's *The Rape of the Fair Country* was marred by all the clichés of the historical novel:

> the only difference is that the glamour and kitsch which are usually devoted to the service of wealth are here lavished upon the poor. It is as if the Deep South of *Gone with the Wind* had undergone a transformation scene, as on a pantomime stage, and reappeared in the South Wales valleys.[41]

Signing off from the *Listener* in the summer of 1959, Rees expressed relief at taking leave of the never-never land of fiction. He spoke too soon: *Encounter* now gave him the chance to applaud Ivy Compton-Burnett's imaginative universe, a mythical world yet real, in which sophistication is allied to violence, wit to passion, and convention to barbarism. Technically, she had gone further than anyone in demonstrating Henry Green's dictum that novelists should eliminate every element of description; what we learn about the characters we learn from their own mouths. Colin MacInnes's *Absolute Beginners* suffered in that respect – 'the world his characters inhabit is not implicit in their actions; it has to be described to us' – yet Rees fully acclaimed a key text of the times, one signalling new freedoms. MacInnes's teenagers had resisted the organized idiocies of their elders: the snobbery, the class system, colour prejudice and sexual inhibition, respect for age and authority. Scratch a MacInnes teenager, said Rees, and you find an old-fashioned working-class socialist (apart from the rejection of sexual puritanism, that is).[42]

By the close of 1959 Rees's prospects had brightened appreciably. Some radio work had arrived, including the translation and adaptation of Brecht's political morality *Die Ausnahme und die Regel* ('The Exception and the Rule') and of Georg Büchner's short novel, *Lenz*; there was even a production of a radio play written by Rees himself, a court-room drama on the moral issues surrounding wider access to atom secrets.[43] Additionally, the *Sunday Times* commissioned six studies of the super-rich, an assignment bringing welcome trips to Germany, France and

Greece. Blending research with personal interview, the resulting pieces were published in early 1960, the year that saw *A Bundle of Sensations*, Rees's first autobiographical volume.

Chapter VI

IN A TEASING PREFACE, REES EXPLAINED THAT *A BUNDLE OF SENSATIONS* could not be a conventional autobiography because he lacked a sense of himself as a continuous, consistent personality; as has been said, he preferred David Hume on personal identity (the self as 'a bundle of different perceptions') to the notion of an inner character or entity which is stable and unchanging. He stressed the multiplicity of the self and that element of the contradictory and unexpected which is absolutely native to our human make-up. In consequence, he would provide a collection of *autobiographies* in which the author's character varied with the circumstances in which it found itself. Though they nod in the direction of philosophy, Rees's musings are best understood in the light of his settled belief that people are not interesting and important for what is personal to them – however fascinating their vagaries might be to themselves – but for what they share with others; consistently he elevated the collective as opposed to the individual experience, his concern being with how men and women are shaped by the objective conditions of the age, by social and historical forces that transcend the individual.

It would have been surprising had Rees, growing up in the depression and with his first-hand experience of fascism, not developed a sense of 'moving in the ambience of history' (to use Lionel Trilling's phrase). In this, he is united with other writers of the 1930s who, as Samuel Hynes has noted, were more than usually generation conscious, favouring autobiographical accounts which would explain their generation's predicament.[44] *A Bundle of Sensations* conforms to this pattern; refreshingly modest in tone, it offers extraordinarily little of a personal nature (next to nothing about love and marriage, about Rees's literary writings or his dramatically fractured career), and in its construction of an imagined self the book frequently presses against the biographical facts. Rees seeks the representative status that would align him with his contemporaries, though in crucial respects he stood apart, even from the left-wing literary intellectuals. By suppression and elimination, by a blending of fictionalized reminiscence and acute social commentary, Rees strives to capture the essence of his times.

The book has as its centre three contrasting chapters on his army experiences: first as the recalcitrant squaddie skiving in the ranks, then as an intelligence officer planning the Dieppe raid, and finally as the soldier-diplomat in end-of-the-war Berlin. Framing this military triptych are two prior chapters (one on his Aberystwyth boyhood, the other on the Silesian visit) and, by way of an epilogue, a meditative account of his convalescence after the motor accident. All six chapters are self-contained, with no bridging passages, and all most beautifully written: Rees's habitual crystalline elegance is flecked with humour and sadness, and not lacking a capacity to move. The opening essay, an expansion of his 1955 radio talk, stands as a peerless evocation of a chapel childhood in Wales. He recalls the evening service in summer:

> The late sunlight used to fall through the tall windows in great golden waves that washed against the green and gilt Corinthian columns that supported the gallery; it was as if sea and the sunset were flooding the chapel. Welsh voices singing raised one and rocked one on a flood of harmony; the air inside the chapel was close and warm and drowsy; I sat in the corner of my pew overwhelmed by some strange bitter-sweet emotion in which happiness and sorrow were equally mixed, while above me in the pulpit the preacher continued to denounce our sins and expound our need of grace. And afterwards we walked through the grey streets of the ugly little town, now crowded with chapelgoers returning home, to Sunday supper at my grandmother's, where my brother and I stared at the Victorian illustrations in the bound copies of *The Quiver* and *The Strand Magazine*, until after supper we all collected round the piano and I stood, half-asleep, holding my mother's hand while we all sang once again the hymns we had sung all day in chapel; until at last the pressure of feeling seemed to grow so

huge within me that I burst into inconsolable, inexplicable tears. My mother kissed me and caressed me, murmuring that I was tired, and took me on her knee where I fell asleep with the tinkling notes of the piano still in my ears. (p. 28)

Reviewers had their favourite chapters (the *TLS* believed that the first German essay gave the reasons for 1939 more clearly than anything in Isherwood), but 'A day at the seaside', Rees's savage dissection of the Dieppe fiasco proved by far the most controversial: it records how Admiral Mountbatten, 'handsome and breezy, like Brighton at its best', had so fully allayed misgivings concerning this doomed operation that it would have proceeded 'even if the troops had been asked to land with no better weapons than their bare hands and fists; in the event, they had very little more'. In contrast, the portrait of Montgomery won universal approval:

One saw a narrow foxy face, long nosed, sharp and intelligent and tenacious, with very bright and clear blue eyes, and a small, light, spare body. The effect was not at all imposing, except for his eyes and an indefinable look in his face of extreme cleverness and sagacity, like a very alert Parson Jack Russell terrier. But what was impressive was an air he had of extraordinary quietness and calm, as if nothing in the world could disturb his peace of mind. He spoke in a quiet voice and his manner, though incisive, was quiet also; one had the feeling that with him everything was in order, like a good housewife whose domestic arrangements are always ready for any conceivable emergency. (pp. 135–6)

Rees stresses the stillness and quietness that everywhere surrounded Montgomery, 'in the study itself, in the entire household, in the garden outside, as if even the birds were under a spell of silence; it was a kind of stillness one would associate more easily with an interview with a priest than a general' (a remarkable insight, judges Montgomery's biographer, Nigel Hamilton).

As for unifying themes within the book, some consensus developed around the view that *A Bundle of Sensations* presents a man, born to an important father, who all his life searched for, and rebelled against, other father figures, both personal and institutional. He had gravitated towards centres of power only to end up in conflict with them. The last chapter signalled a change: becalmed in a hospital ward, Rees himself begins to feel paternal.

The book seemed a brilliant beginning to a new career as professional writer. Then, amid the success (immediate sales of 2,600), Rees succumbed to the depressive illness that had dogged him over the years. A psychiatrist's report on his breakdown spoke of guilt and shame at having let down his father and family. It is Revd Rees who dominates the opening of the book, and, as if to condition Goronwy's thinking on personal identity, he harbours a dual nature, one part terrifying to his son. For on Sundays this most reasonable and tolerant of men was 'quite suddenly transformed into a kind of witch-doctor, demoniac and possessed; it was as if, without warning, he had gone off his head'. The child gazes at him 'high in the pulpit, towering over me, a huge black figure, angry and eloquent, its arms out-stretched like the wings of a great bird . . . preaching endlessly on the tremendous themes of sin, grace, redemption, and eternal punishment'. Yet Rees *père* was as God to Goronwy, who in some ways remained for ever after a child of the chapel. In the closing hospital chapter his Puritan conscience afflicts him over aspects of his past; these resurface in night-time hallucinations of being steeped in vice and crime and of desperately needing to escape, or else be faced with 'terrible exposure and shame'. Here, one might speculate, is Rees's guilt at having succumbed to Burgess; the nightmare world is Burgess's, specifically his Mayfair flat: the sinister drinking den with a room above, 'half brothel and half doss-house, of extraordinary squalor and dreariness'.

A year after *A Bundle of Sensations*, Rees produced for Chatto & Windus a book revision of his *Sunday Times* pieces on the super-rich. They lent themselves to a rewarding study in so much as his original selection – J. Paul Getty, Sir Simon Marks, Aristotle

Onassis, Alfred Krupp, Charles Clore and Marcel Boussec – spanned a range of nationalities and a variety of commercial enterprises. Though the portraits made good reading, *The Multi-Millionaires: Six Studies in Wealth* (1961) gained from an additional afterword taking stock of the seriously rich. Are they, as Hemingway would have it, different from us only in their degree of wealth? Rees finds them dull dogs (apart from Sir Simon Marks), with no instinct for pleasure and little aptitude for domestic life. Mr Millions comes to life in his counting house, thus exemplifying the biblical proposition that where your treasure is, there will your heart be also. Quite simply, he loves his business, and his stunning success is the outcome of a rare temperamental make-up: one which combines the miser's spirit of thrift and calculation with the recklessness of the gambler. Again, *The Multi-Millionaires* sold well and on the back of this second success Rees signed a contract with Weidenfeld & Nicolson for a book on salons and hostesses. Sadly, this came to nothing, as did the book on Burgess he had promised Chatto & Windus. More seriously, his lucrative work for the *Sunday Times* dried up. The early 1960s were becoming Rees's most painful years: his financial problems multiplied, his father (long since in retirement near Witney) died in his ninety-fifth year, and Rees's depressive illness would not be shaken off.

Surprisingly, in the midst of this came two short stories, Rees's only foray into fiction subsequent to *Where No Wounds Were*. 'Hermes', centred on an ingenious and amusing Greek working as an agent for the British during the war, became a radio play (it was broadcast on the Third Programme, 28 March 1964), while 'The horsemen' appeared in *London Magazine* in April 1964. This second story concerns a group of British army officers stationed in post-war Germany. Socially prejudiced and politically reactionary, they are pictured through the eyes of Cliff, of Yorkshire farming stock and judged a social inferior:

> They seemed to me sad and sour and bad tempered. Even their laughter had something malicious about it. Their lives had gone

wrong, and they dimly felt that the same thing was happening to people like themselves all over the world. In Germany they were, still, for the moment, masters; but already they knew that it would not last for long and they wished to enjoy it while it did last, and they hated and resented anyone who might deprive them of this last taste of empire. They looked on England as a lover who had betrayed them, they felt lonely and abandoned; for a moment it struck me that, despite their medal ribbons and their uniforms, their Sam Brownes and their moustaches, there was something intensely feminine about them all.

To Cliff's surprise, these officers with whom he is billeted hit it off quite naturally with a band of Ukrainian 'displaced persons', all through a day spent riding together. The Anglo-Russian fiesta has been organized by Cliff, an enthusiastic horseman himself, who now becomes acceptable to the senior military circle. Rees's story reflects an understanding gathered first at Oxford, that it is not the individual which English society excludes, but rather the social and intellectual forms which are not compatible with its own assumptions. 'It's a funny thing, Cliff,' says Colonel Warburton in retirement, 'but before that day I never really liked you. Thought you were a bit of a prig – stand-offish, if you know what I mean.'

Away from fiction, Rees relied on *Encounter* as an outlet for some substantial essays. 'Have the Welsh a future?' (March 1964) is less an exercise in crystal-gazing than a personal retracing of the past. Once more Rees returns to his boyhood in Aberystwyth, the very citadel of traditional culture. He knew little else of Wales until at the age of thirteen he met some lads from the Valleys on an annual summer camp. It was a defining moment:

> To me they seemed like creatures of another race, bigger, rougher, tougher, uncouth and barbarian, jeering and foul-mouthed; I might have been an ancient Roman confronted for the first time by the Goths. But they also seemed freer and more adult and less inhibited than the boys I had known, scornful of authority, untouched by the miasma of bigotry and hypocrisy which emanated from the twenty-four chapels of our little town.

He stresses the traumatic shock of his family's move to south Wales, where he encountered an industrial community in the throes of the great depression: a community which soon came to stand for everything that was best in Wales. 'It seemed to me then that all the virtues, if such indeed they were, of the Welsh way of life were worth nothing compared with the efforts and struggles of the South Wales Miners' Federation.' This remained Rees's settled perspective, that of an ossified north and west, the world of the Welsh intelligentsia wedded to their communal myths and with no capacity for self-criticism, and of an industrial south whose resources – political, intellectual and spiritual – owed nothing to traditional Welsh culture, as it had become.

With his own family history in mind, Rees surveyed the legacy of that culture at its finest: a common language, a widely disseminated literary life and a fundamentally democratic disposition – something which still made the Welsh feel alien in class-infected England. All flowed from a form of religion by which the Welsh, no less than the Jews, became a people of the book, astonishingly literate, 'literate perhaps even to the point of oversophistication, so that nowhere in the world is the word more easily taken for the deed'. Rees praised the Welsh achievement in education (university colleges accessible to the poorest) and the Welsh political radicalism which had galvanized British Liberalism and produced in David Lloyd George a politician of genius: one truly representative, both in his early triumph and later decline, of the Welsh rural culture that bred him. But,

> a people cannot live upon its past, and that past itself, however well loved, ceases to have any meaning unless it is continuously transformed and transmuted in the light of the present. This is a task which modern Wales has conspicuously failed to discharge, and the responsibility for this failure falls pre-eminently upon those who would claim to be its spiritual and intellectual leaders, who, having little virtue in themselves, continue to live on the little that is left of the faith and energy of their fathers.

This was a passage applauded by Harri Webb in a spirited nationalist riposte.[45] He believed that Welsh nationalists would endorse much of what Rees had said, as Webb himself had done when two months previously he had spoken of the Welsh way of life as mostly 'junk' – with the Welsh language 'a treasure on the scrap-heap'. Rees's thoughts on the language came by way of his comments in the essay on a report by the Council of Wales and Monmouthshire (*The Welsh Language Today*); this, so he felt, was a characteristically Welsh document, 'full of the illusions and evasions which make any serious discussion of the Welsh language almost impossible within Wales'. Its assertion that all Welshmen were proud of the language and wished to see it survive was palpably false ('how can a man be genuinely proud of what means nothing to him?'); no national unity existed around the language, so that when the council expressed its belief that this 'unity' need not be disrupted, it was simply hoping that no one would be rash enough to offer any serious criticism of the policies it advocated. At heart, Rees looked on Welsh as the language of a dying world, resisted in the ascendant south and therefore inevitably doomed. But Rees, Webb insisted, had simply lost touch with a changing Wales; he had ignored the widespread campaign to grant Welsh official status and the efforts of parents in the Anglicized south to establish Welsh-language schools there. Severe on the myths of others, Rees nursed his own romantic illusions about the industrialized areas and the iron curtain along the Brecon Beacons that separated them from the backward rest of Wales – a part of the country deemed somehow less contemporary, less real. And the notion that south Wales miners had more in common with those in the Ruhr than with their rural countrymen was plain 'doctrinaire silliness'. This said, Webb granted that Rees had made a serious contribution to the national debate; at least here was a Welshman who identified with his nation, and Wales, 'which has a future, needs us all. It would even need Goronwy Rees, in which case he has a future too.'

In passing, Webb gave assent to what he saw as Rees's 'unsentimental dismissal of Aneurin Bevan as a relic of the past'.

This calls for clarification. Rees had written about Bevan in a review of Michael Foot's biography, a book judged a failure all the sadder because 'Bevan had a force and vivacity of character, a liveliness of imagination and a quickness of intelligence, a breadth of mind and warmth of heart, which are given to few politicians'.[46] As if in a vision, Bevan had seen the face of capitalism revealed in the poverty and misery of the depression; it had the mark of the beast, and henceforth he would interpret the world in accordance with his vision. While this gave him a comprehensive view of politics, it prevented him from understanding how scientific and industrial developments would change the nature of capitalism, creating conditions largely tolerable for the proletariat. Rees mentioned one other aspect of Bevan's career: how almost single-handedly he had prevented Churchill during the war from attaining some kind of parliamentary dictatorship. The stand brought him public obloquy yet, as the 1945 election made clear, Bevan was 'often much closer to the feelings of those who were actually fighting on the battlefields than to those who were so ready to impugn his patriotism'.

At the beginning of 'Have the Welsh a future?', Rees touched upon the question of national self-government. In the 1930s he had urged a parliament of Wales and this remained his position. However, complete political severance from Westminister was not a realistic option. Though set apart from the English, by race, culture, social structure and temperament, the Welsh were none-theless too commonsensical ever to be persuaded that they suffered under an evil that only total independence would remove. And it was as a commonsensical Welshman that he responded to an *Encounter* request (January 1961) for his views on Britain's possible entry into the Common Market. Rees welcomed the move, and expressly as a transition towards a more comprehensive political union. True, the Common Market would restrict Britain's sovereignty, but 'unrestricted sover-eignty, even when British made, had not been a blessing in the world'; in any case, such sovereignty was largely a myth, capable of breeding dangerous illusions. Rees belonged to a people who had long ago lost their national independence, though not their national identity; both Wales and Britain had thereby gained, and he felt certain that similar benefits would follow, both for Britain and Europe, from a British surrender of sovereignty to the community of Europe. At bedrock Rees believed in a European cultural commingling, in 'the community of ideas that once had stretched from London to Warsaw'.

This he made explicit in a wonderfully atmospheric essay occasioned by a visit to Prague for a Kafka exhibition (*Encounter*, September 1964). How to interpret this improbable commemoration? – for surely no writer was less fitted for admittance to the communist literary canon. What struggles lay behind this apparent acceptance? What arguments in Kafka's favour? The bookshops of Prague stocked none of his writings, neither in the original nor in translation. It is claimed that the demand is so strong that they immediately sell out, or so weak (for a German writer in a Czech city) that booksellers are naturally reluctant to stock him. Rees picks out among the hoardings an advertisement for the exhibition: a poster-size photograph of the author, with the words 'Franz Kafka' and nothing more. 'There is something inexpressibly elegant and distinguished, like his own prose, in his stance and attitude, in his smile, in his eyes which gaze at one from some immense distance, which is more than the distance of time.' Mystery surrounds the whereabouts of the exhibition, as it does the manner of its subject's rehabilitation; Rees has stumbled into Kafka's very own world in which nothing is precisely what it seems. However great his interest in the exhibition, he must not expect to visit it easily. Eventually he tracks it down to the Strahov, a small gallery off the entrance to a monastery, where the same Kafka poster welcomes a trickle of visitors. The exhibition itself was the outcome of a Kafka conference held outside Prague a year previously. There scholars had variously argued for Kafka as the critic of capitalism, as an enemy of the bureaucracy that Czechoslovakia was at last throwing off, or not for any political reason at all, but as a great European writer who like Proust and Joyce should be granted 'a permanent visitor's visa'. Rees charts a Prague mediated by the writer, a cultural meeting place at the centre of Europe that gave rise to Kafka's particular world: an amalgam of the Czech, the German and above all the Jewish, in which each element was transmuted by the presence of the others. With the Jewish ghetto liquidated and Kafka's circle persecuted out of existence, his spirit alone survives, waiting to be embraced by the socialist countries.

Rees half-looked on the communist world through the eyes of a man of the 1930s, still possessed of the irrational feeling that this world was somehow new and progressive. He observes its outward face in Prague's smartest hotels,

> where in the dining-room flocks of waitresses, plump and ruddy as if they had come straight off the land, in black dresses and frilled white aprons, their trays held high aloft on upturned palms, pass in endless procession like figures on some Egyptian frieze, under the eyes of an inexorable head waiter in snowy white waistcoat and tailcoat; where in the evenings couples dance to a string orchestra playing 'Down Mexico Way' and the *jeunesse dorée* of Prague self-consciously perform a modified version of the Twist in which vitality has been wholly sacrificed to decorum.

The communist élite adopt a style long since vanished in the West; here it is the past, not the future, which beckons. Away from Prague's central thoroughfares Rees enters 'a desert of silence and desolation', akin to that which he beheld when, from an observation platform, he overlooked the Berlin Wall and gazed into the eastern sector. On an earlier *Encounter* assignment (April 1964) he came face to face with the Wall, 'the most naked assertion . . . that life was not intended to be anything except nasty, brutish and short'. Scabrous blotches mottled the porous grey concrete 'like symptoms of a disease'; they had seeped through from the other side, which was whitewashed so that any movement close to it, across the *Todeszone*, the unobstructed zone of death, might be more easily detected. He takes a train to East Berlin and in the bleak halls of the Friedrichstrasse waits with a knot of travellers for his passport to be checked. Armed guards of the people's police study every page, with the result that he too comes to regard the document 'with a kind of awe and reverence which it had never inspired before'. Here again is Kafkaland, 'something in the atmosphere, something threatening, which makes one feel that issues are at stake and that laughter would have appalling consequences'.

A lifelong interest in Germany, in its literature, philosophy and politics, continually surfaced in Rees. His Welsh pieces by contrast were sporadic, though one novelist in particular excited him, and for reasons not difficult to imagine. Emyr Humphreys possesssed 'an instinctive sense of the ways in which men and women were shaped by their environment'. *Outside the House of Baal* had proper ambition in its social and historical scope and was sustained by a marvellous accuracy of detail and an accomplished formal technique: 'The effect is more pictorial than narrative or dramatic, as of some large elaborately composed fresco, the whole suffused by the elegiac light of a Claude, but each detail painted with the sharp and loving clarity of some Dutch master.' Rees's *Spectator* notice (14 May 1965) became a keynote assessment, providing handsome dust-jacket copy for Humphreys's novels over the years. The review distanced Humphreys from what previously Rees had described as 'the fatal Welsh instinct for sentimentalizing, sweetening, and vulgarizing whatever is best in their own people': it had turned the richly endowed Gwyn Thomas, a man of the Rhondda ('at once flamboyant and repressed, boisterous and melancholy, pious and blaspheming, passionate and cynical'), through lack of discipline and self-criticism, into a literary *farceur*, some sort of licensed clown. (Rees's asides on the Anglo-Welsh are acute, as when he speaks of 'a kind of compassionate mockery' as the feeling behind *Under Milk Wood*.)

For the remainder of the 1960s Rees turned to the well-paying Weidenfeld & Nicolson for a mixture of non-literary books. First came *The Rhine* (1967), a highbrow historical guide, carelessly compiled and strongest on politics and literature. *St Michael: A History of Marks and Spencer* (1969) dates back to *The Multi-*

Millionaires and its chapter on Sir Simon Marks, the company's chairman of forty years. Rees greatly admired Sir Simon Marks, who in turn encouraged Rees to write the company history, granting him a handsome retainer to make this possible, along with a comfortable berth in the new Baker Street offices. It was a world which fascinated Rees; he accompanied Sir Simon on his company visits ('like a very good battalion commander carrying out an inspection') and drafted his chairman's speeches. *St Michael* veers towards hagiology – Marks and Spencer as a characteristically Jewish concern, transcending the limits of business and evolving into a general philosophy of enterprise and human relations of significance to society as a whole – but Rees's factual research was thorough and ably presented, and a paperback edition was called for in 1973.

His third book for Weidenfeld & Nicolson was a more ambitious affair. *The Great Slump: Capitalism in Crisis, 1929–33* attempted to describe and to explain the phenomenon of the great depression, that international economic crisis which began with the Wall Street crash of 1929 and came to a close, according to Rees, in 1933 with Roosevelt's inauguration as president and Hitler's assumption of power. Confining his account to three leading countries – the United States, Germany and Britain – Rees considered the capitalist breakdown not exclusively in terms of economics but within the social and political conditions which had produced it; as A. J. P. Taylor observed, besides his technical grasp of financial systems, Rees had a real feel for the period, having lived through it himself. It was the great depression, Rees suggested, more than the Great War, that 'fixed a gulf between what went before and what came after; . . . like some seismological disturbance it shifted the ground on which men stood'. A contribution to a specialist field, *The Great Slump* is neverthless accessible, with much vivid detail and a breadth of literary reference. Reviewers generally welcomed it, despite its frequent inaccuracies; Rees was 'a somewhat slapdash historian', A. J. P. Taylor had to agree (for this project he had no research assistant to rely upon, as had been the case with *St Michael*).

Chapter VII

REES'S FINAL PHASE MIGHT BE SAID TO HAVE BEGUN IN FEBRUARY 1966 when he joined the advisory board of *Encounter*, a prestigious politico-cultural monthly whose worldwide sales at that time came close to 40,000. The journal had thrown him a lifeline as others were turning their backs and now its joint editor Stephen Spender introduced him to Melvin Lasky, his American counterpart in a bi-national editorial arrangement. The ex-Trotskyist Lasky immediately took to Rees, agreeing that he become a contributing editor, with a regular monthly column: 'I admired and I liked him; he was enormously talented and he represented the spirit of the magazine.' *Encounter* indeed became a spiritual home; Rees liked its Jewish-American tough-mindedness, its cosmopolitan breadth (a balance of distinguished contributors from Britain, America, Europe and beyond), and its desire to break down the departmentalization of literature and politics. Moreover, he endorsed the anti-communist bias that *Encounter* displayed from the beginning.

Nominally published by Secker and Warburg, and sponsored by the Paris-based Congress for Cultural Freedom, the periodical took up its position in the long ideological battle waged between the Soviet Union and the West. This said, there was no precise *Encounter* line, or so its editors argued; rather, in Stephen Spender's formulation, its political aim was

> to provide a platform for the greatest possible amount of disagreement within a broad area of agreement. We are agreed that in the present state of the world, democracy provides the basis for individual freedom that is denied under Communist and other dictatorships: and that therefore this freedom should be exercised, maintained, and defended. (*Encounter*, January 1962)

Widely admired for its literary achievements, the journal disturbed some critics on account of its political partiality, and the appearance of a weighty anthology from the first ten years of publication gave them the chance to say so. In the *New Statesman* (20 December 1963) Conor Cruise O'Brien remarked that *Encounter* conveyed the impression that its propaganda was no propaganda at all, even though almost every issue contained some cleverly written material favourable to the United States and hostile to the Soviet Union. He broached this subject again in a New York lecture in 1966, this time bolstered by revelations that *Encounter* had once been funded by the Central Intelligence Agency, using the ostensibly independent Congress for Cultural Freedom as a conduit. Airing these disclosures, O'Brien spoke of an *Encounter* tactic whereby

> writers of high achievement and complete integrity were led unconsciously to validate, through their collaboration, the more purposeful activities of lesser writers who in turn were engaged in a sustained and consistent political activity in the interests – and it now appears at the expense – of the power structure in Washington.

In his column of August 1966 Rees dismissed such a claim as nonsense, and, incensed by a bitter exchange with O'Brien at the beginning of 1965, he launched an intemperate attack on his adversary's character and writing. Libel proceedings ensued, as did further revelations of the clandestine CIA–*Encounter* connection – with the consequence that the journal had no option but to apologize for an unwarranted outburst.[47] Frank Kermode, Spender's successor as English editor, felt compelled to resign, while others on the British Left became permanently estranged from a publication which, professing openness and independence of thought, had dealt in concealment and deception. (The stain proved ineradicable; *Encounter* from this point on seemed less than the sum of its parts, with no shortage of talent or resources, yet strangely lacking in influence.)

After the initial discomfort Rees flourished in his post. American subvention was nothing to be ashamed of: it was a

The Encounter *columnist R. 'He kept his literary talent, his gift for friendship, and his almost uncanny perceptiveness' (A. J. Ayer).*

kind of intellectual Marshall Plan designed to strengthen the West's tradition of free debate and enquiry at a time when this was under severe attack from the Soviet bloc. He understood how in 1953, with the continent exhausted by war and the states of central Europe already lost to Soviet communism, one might have believed that core European values were in danger of being extinguished: 'There were also many who were not sorry if this were so, especially those militant spirits mobilised in Europe's great fifth column, the communist parties of the West; they were waiting for the death of Europe.'[48] Britain's own fifth column remained Rees's obsession; in 1963 (the year of Kim Philby's defection), he disclosed to investigating journalists his convictions about Blunt – but Blunt was on the verge of a deal promising him immunity from prosecution. His relationship to Blunt he saw reflected in the case of Alger Hiss, the United States government official accused by Whittaker Chambers (then senior editor of *Time* magazine) of having been a communist agent during the 1930s, part of an espionage network (it included Chambers) operating from government positions of power. The case fascinated Rees, who never for a moment doubted that Chambers had told the truth. In a powerful *Spectator* review (22 January 1965), he examined Chambers's character, or rather, its demonization by American and British commentators. For, if Alger Hiss was an angel, the spotless all-American hero, there was something diabolical about Chambers, the spy-turned-informer whose show of new-found religion masked a moral decay. 'One came straight out of Henry James, the other from Dostoievsky. Who could doubt which of them one would choose to have as a friend, or in which to place one's trust?' Except that it was the demon whom the jury believed. Rees identified with Chambers, in the ex-communist's act of testimony and in all his consequent sufferings, and he rounded on Chambers's enemies, Conor Cruise O'Brien especially;[49] he and others of the intellectual Left, not communists themselves but disliking anti-communists, had sought to destroy this testimony through a campaign of character assassination. O'Brien's attack on Chambers touched Rees on the raw, so that when in the New York lecture O'Brien turned his fire on *Encounter* Rees could not contain himself.

During his early *Encounter* period Rees completed his clutch of commissions: the Rhineland guide, the Marks and Spencer history, his study of the depression and an edition for Heron Books of Koestler's *Darkness at Noon* (1970); lavishly illustrated, the latter contained an outstanding commentary by Rees. Then came *A Chapter of Accidents* (1972), a second volume of memoirs which, together with *A Bundle of Sensations*, stands as his finest achievement. Like the earlier book, it dates back to Aberystwyth and the mid-1950s when Rees began his extended reminiscence of Burgess. By 1959 – after the disastrous reworkings printed in the *People* – he proposed recasting the material as fiction, and went so far as to accept an advance for a novel about Burgess and Maclean. Ten years later talk had turned to another volume of memoirs, to be 'both a chapter of autobiography and a reflection of English (and also Welsh) life between 1930 and 1955'. The text as eventually published measures up to Rees's prospectus. The central section is very largely a straight narrative of Rees's relations with Burgess, from their first meeting at Oxford to the moment in 1951 when Burgess defected to Moscow. This is followed by a concluding account, increasingly sardonic in tone, of the aftermath of the Burgess affair, that disastrous phase in Rees's life culminating in the expulsion from Aberystwyth. However, it was always Rees's contention that Burgess, though extraordinary and fascinating as a psychological case, was also a social human being, bred out of a specific environment and a process of education associated with it. Of course, Rees thought the same of himself, and in consequence he provided two extended initial chapters – one on his boyhood in Wales, the other on his undergraduate Oxford – in which he explored two highly dissimilar worlds: two kinds of life and society which (so it is implied) he and Burgess in large part reflected and embodied.

The pages on his childhood are lit by love and affection towards his parents, his school and its teachers; behind them lay a culture which elevated concern for others, not simply for their material well-being but for their spiritual and intellectual needs as well. What was abroad in Welsh society was distilled within his family. There was a time for the evening under lamplight: the scene, here rendered with a wonderful emotional delicacy, was one which came to possess Rees as emblematic of the age-old security of home, a place of books and learning; and books were at the centre of his life and his apprehension of the world around him:

> During my last year at school I worked extremely hard, especially in the long winter evenings when I sat bent over my books at the table in our parlour while my mother and father read in silence in their arm-chairs on either side of the fireplace. The crimson tablecloth on which my books were piled, the glowing light of the fire, fed by the best Welsh coal, the dark mahogany furniture and the Victorian prints on the walls, the scratching of my pen on the paper, the absolute and unbroken silence, induced in me a feeling that time had come to a stop and that we three were preserved for ever in an immobility which change could never threaten. And I was happy that it should be so, for the quiet room with its shadows in the corner where the lamplight never penetrated was transformed into a kind of enchanted cave peopled by all the spirits called up from the past by my books, which I read as if they were works of necromancy that could endow me with magical powers. If I paused for a moment and looked up from my reading, the sense of being encapsuled in some timeless moment, of total and absolute insulation against everything that existed outside those four walls, was so intense that I seemed to float free of my body and look down on the room as if it were one of those Dutch interiors in which every worn and familiar object, and the faces of those who sit among them, are illuminated by an internal light, a warmth, a glow, a splendour that came from some world which is beyond the world of change. (p. 54)

Not that Rees's Welsh world was homogeneous. By his own admission, the young man who arrived at New College was a complex, contradictory character, prone to sullenness and out-bursts of temper. He would seem to have internalized a whole Welsh cultural psychodrama, wherein the traditional world of his father – rural, Welsh-speaking, Liberal-Nonconformist – clashed with the industrial south, a heavily Anglicized community driven by radical socialism. As we have seen, Rees fiercely identified with the latter – even as he confessed that his thoughts of revolution were coloured by biblical imagery absorbed in childhood. He remembered a Welsh hymn about the survivors of Armageddon; like them, the men and women of the valleys would inherit a world made new after the overthrow of capitalism, agent of doom and evil. Art, poetry, literature, revolution – these were the elements of the fantasy world Rees had built for himself at Cardiff and which he hoped he might share with others at Oxford. There he did find friends who were enthusiasts of art and literature, more especially in his second year when he began to forget the many things that divided him from his fellow undergraduates. For he was not, he felt, of Oxford, no matter how gladly he succumbed to its infinitely seductive appeal. He was the outsider looking in, and, as he became more acclimatized, the insider looking out, 'teetering deliciously between two societies to neither of which was I really attached'. The alien eye is sharpest on the homosexual attitudes that dominated the Oxford of his day, a tone and disposition owing much to G. E. Moore's pronouncements on the primacy of art and personal relationships, and perhaps best encapsulated in E. M. Forster's 'Only connect' (it was by quoting Forster that Blunt sought to dissuade Rees from denouncing Burgess to MI5). Whatever the philosophical ballast, the cult of personal relationships found ready adherents among young men of English public-school background. Not many were overtly homosexual; rather, they displayed an indifference, and sometimes an active hostility, to the company of women; and it was not, so Rees came to see, conducive to public welfare that the country be governed by a class formed under conditions which approximated to 'a badly conducted monastery'.

Hugh Trevor-Roper, for one, thought Rees's social analysis perceptive and just. 'Nowhere have I read a better exposure of "the liberal illusion" of the 1930s . . . as literature and as autobiography this book is unique', ran his review of *A Chapter of Accidents*. Others were equally impressed: Michael Foot spoke of a tale superbly told, 'with a suave and subtle brilliance which carries all before it'; Geoffrey Grigson – never an easy man to please – found the book 'extraordinarily occupying and suggestive'; while to Philip Toynbee it was 'as full of fine *obiter dicta* as . . . of vivid descriptions'. Richard Crossman questioned Rees's reading of political history and the periodically evasive account of his relations with Burgess; even so, 'Treated as a *nouvelle* – fiction based on fact – it is without doubt a minor masterpiece' (both he and Noël Annan agreed that the Burgess portrait was masterly).[50] There was one fierce dissenter, enraged by the book's treatment of Wales: what for English critics was brilliant social analysis was for Harri Webb the 'obsessive chronicles of snobbery, sodomy and treachery'; the author resembled 'nothing so much as an ageing daughter of the night . . . parading in the pathetic finery of a bygone day on some windy corner long deserted by the traffic of pleasure'. Rees took offence at this *Planet* review (May 1972), to the point of threatening legal action; and he must have been particularly repelled by a reference to one of his early Oxford friends, the German patriot Adam von Trott, executed for his part in the plot to assassinate Hitler. Webb likened Rees to Trott, the man 'who played with fire and only had himself to blame for getting burnt, an empty character, with no loyalty or sensibility'. (Rees had handsomely saluted Trott and the many other Germans who had fought against Hitler: they 'had dedicated to Germany a love which surpassed the love of country'.)

Rees authored one more book – a privately printed company history of the multinational corporation, Dalgety (for which he received £15,000 plus expenses) – and edited one other: *McVicar by Himself* (1974), the prison writings of John McVicar, a commission that came Rees's way following an *Encounter* article on the dubious efficacy of long-term imprisonment. Judging McVicar's manuscripts 'a considerable literary achievement', Rees dwelt in his introduction on the 'machismo' which McVicar believed was the basis of his own criminality. Far from exposing that machismo as 'a kind of romantic illusion, a form of false consciousness', McVicar's experience of long-term imprisonment reinforced it. His change of mind and heart (his 'conversion', as it struck Rees) arose from the discovery of 'a higher order and value' in the life he was able to live with his wife and child following his sensational escape from Durham. Rees edited the manuscript independently, having been refused permission to visit the author in prison, but the two met face to face some time after the appearance of the book (a work which in the author's opinion would not have been published but for Rees); McVicar and his wife had parted, though he still remained close to his son – the decisive influence in what Rees had described (McVicar thought correctly) as his 'conversion'.

For fully fourteen years Rees proved an *Encounter* dependable, filing his monthly 3,000 words for a column signed simply *R*. Once in a while he submitted an additional extended essay but 'Column' was his permanent platform, from which he might expatiate on any subject of his choosing. Introducing *Brief Encounters* (1974), a collection of his pieces from the years 1966–72, Rees outlined the problems facing a monthly columnist: how one had to write at least six weeks ahead of publication, trying to maintain some contact with events as they occurred yet conscious that a topic, inviting at the moment, might be as dead as mutton by the time the words appeared. As it happened, such constrictions worked in Rees's favour, drawing him repeatedly to long-standing fields of interest. Germany is a case in point. Germanist and philo-Semite, he had known the country both before and after Hitler's seizure of power, and a number of his *Encounter* pieces survey the puzzles and paradoxes of this turbulent period:[51] intense intellectual and artistic vitality set beside social decadence and the growth of National Socialism; the extent to which Weimar culture was expressive of a peculiarly Jewish spirit; above all, the bewildering phenomenon of Hitler and how precisely he could be related to Germany's past. On a personal note, Rees recollected Hitler's brand of oratory, experienced with 10,000 others at the *Sportpalast* in Berlin:

> It is of the kind that speaks neither to the mind nor the heart of his audience, but plays upon its nerves until they are strung to such a pitch of intensity that they shriek for release in action. It was the kind of oratory that, in my childhood, was capable of transforming an incurable alcoholic into a life-long teetotaller in the twinkling of an eyelid. But it can only be practised by one who has a profound and subtle understanding of the secret hopes and fears of his audience . . . Who knows, if I had not been inoculated in childhood against the tricks of oratory, I might have succumbed myself.[52]

Surveying developments in the Soviet Union, Rees saw no radical break with the Stalinist past. The Khruschev dawn was a false one; the regime remained an absolute evil though its seductive powers were waning, and with them, the immense intellectual and spiritual prestige that Soviet communism once enjoyed in the West. He celebrated milestones in the undermining of communism's moral claims: first came *Darkness at Noon* ('the Communist Party never looked the same again'), then in 1968 Robert Conquest's *The Great Terror* ('in the long run his book will have a profound and permanent effect on public opinion'). Soviet splits and purges and dissension within its satellites had persuaded many witnesses to break their silence, and most significant of all, the flood of *samizdat* literature was evidence of the growing movement of internal intellectual opposition. Rees greatly admired the dissidents, who in turn were grateful to him ('the only Westerner to be quoted at length in the Soviet underground press', noted Robert Conquest).[53] Rees's interview with Valery Tarsis (April 1966) offered no grounds for believing that the Soviet Union was evolving towards a more humane and liberal society; the dissident writer's testimony gave room only for 'a vast and tragic perspective of millions of men and women, huge cities, immense spaces, controlled by a degenerate and dying state in which decay has gone so far that it has lost all confidence in itself'.

But Solzhenitsyn was Rees's hero, a writer who met all his expectations of a major novelist working in the great Russian and European tradition. Solzhenitsyn was a representative figure; his experiences reflected those of millions of his people. He told the truth about their lives, which was the truth about Russia itself. And his work showed something more than simple opposition to Soviet communism: it affirmed a faith in the dignity of man and the moral worth of the individual. Thus it struck a note not of despair but of hope, of optimism even, since Solzhenitsyn assured us that even under the conditions of the Archipelago the human spirit survives. 'He comes very near to saying that *only* in the Archipelago, where men are stripped of everything in which they have found something to comfort, sustain or distract them, can the human spirit find that peace and freedom in which it is naturally born to live.'[54] It was not a message that found easy acceptance in the West, any more than it did in the Soviet empire: 'For it is essentially a religious message; and fundamentally *The Gulag Archipelago* is not a political book but a religious one' (October 1974). Solzhenitsyn's message became yet more unpalatable when, after 1974, the deported writer turned his anger against the United States. The West had lost its moral purpose in face of Soviet evil: thus the disarray and confusion surrounding the policy of *détente*. 'People quickly get tired of martyrs, particularly when they have the bad taste to survive their martyrdom', reflected Rees on Solzhenitsyn's falling stock (September 1976). He remained as unqualified in his admiration as he had been in 1971, when he lashed the *TLS* over its insistence that Solzhenitsyn's Nobel Prize was a cold-war ploy of the West's, for which we had to apologize before we could expect any softening of official Soviet attitudes towards the writer. Rees was appalled – it was 'shameful and horrifying' that the *TLS* should grovel before the KGB (January 1971). The KGB, we now know, used enormous resources in an effort to discredit Solzhenitsyn following the award of the prize. Their concern was not misplaced: 'the most total and absolute condemnation of the Soviet regime that has ever been written', confirmed Rees of *The*

Gulag Archipelago; 'its publication has probably been the greatest single blow ever delivered against the prestige of the Soviet Union' (September 1978).

Implicit in cold warriordom was support for the United States, though in years disturbed and darkened by the war in Vietnam this could never be unquestioning. Faced with widespread anti-Americanism in western intellectual circles, Rees strove to make intelligible 'the contradictions between what . . . Americans are at heart and what their government does in their name and what they do in the service of their government'.[55] Nine months before he died, he felt it true to say that whatever the shortcomings of democracy in America, 'they are as nothing compared with the crimes that have been and continue to be committed in the name of Communism' (March 1978). The judgement appeared in a review of a book by Diana Trilling, a friend in the 1960s who came to discern the nub of Rees's political interest. She writes that she was continually astonished by his knowledge of the political culture of the United States, or rather, of that sphere which is now referred to as 'cultural politics' – 'that area of our political discourse which bears most directly upon ideas and principles and upon the moral life of the nation'.[56] Rees believed that to this sphere the greatest writers brought an imaginative understanding of the processes that made their national life what it was. He found such a quality of understanding in Norman Mailer, and to a degree in Gore Vidal. The latter's *Burr* was an accurate reflection on the early years of the republic, Rees claiming that from the very beginning there had been in the United States 'a compulsion towards territorial dominion, an imperial theme so powerful that it disdained all moral and constitutional restraints, and dragged all Presidents in its wake, whatever their professed political beliefs and objectives' (May 1974).

Writers feature regularly in Rees's *Encounter* column, European writers preponderantly and André Malraux more than once. Rees's comments on *Antimémoires* say much about his own autobiographical writings. 'Of what interest to me is anything, if it only interests me?', is the question pondered by Malraux, advocating a form of autobiography that is not a personal confession but a record of events carrying a wider public significance. How much the Gaullist minister still retained the habits of thought of the young Marxist and revolutionary, Rees observed (January 1968), conscious of a similar legacy in his own thinking about literature (it lingered as well in his loyalty to the Welsh working class, and in his willingness to conceive of a Eurocommunism not of the petrified Soviet kind). As for English writers, Rees published some incisive pieces on the political stance of writers of the Auden generation.[57] He dismissed the notion that they were cynical Marxists and communists who knew what Stalin was up to, and fully approved of it. The comparison with Brecht was instructive; 'it was impossible to talk to Brecht without at once realising what an intellectual and emotional abyss divided him from our English literary comrades'. For their mental habits were ineradicably English: pragmatic, empirical and sceptical, and obstinately resistant to those large, universal, metaphysical and philosophical systems that found favour on the continent. 'Somehow, for the English reality keeps breaking in, and, in the '30s, it was the specifically English reality which so stubbornly refused to conform to the Marxist scenario.' The radicalism of the English writers derived from no political or economic analysis but was an emotional and cultural reaction against a spiritually sick society, a civilization shattered by one war and threatened by another to come. Of the poor they knew next to nothing, though the poor as victims had a part to play in a writer's mythology. For above all, they were writers at the outset of their careers; those who came off best – Auden, Isherwood, MacNeice – were able to maintain some kind of distance between themselves and the events of the time, while others, like Day-Lewis and Spender, for a while 'sacrificed their literary integrity to a political cause of which they knew little and understood less'. (Rees noted how the literary work of the once derided Bright Young Things – Waugh, Green, Powell, Betjeman – showed a greater staying power than did so much of the 'committed' literature of the 1930s.)

One can here do no more than skim the surface of Rees's *Encounter* journalism, over 400,000 words in all, the bulk reflecting British social and political preoccupations during the 1960s and 1970s. *Brief Encounters* displays some favourite early themes: education and the universities; the counter-culture and the cult of permissiveness ('what the permissive society chiefly permits is an unlimited liberty to talk nonsense'); the condition of the media (Pope's goddess Dulness still reducing 'life, society, literature, art, to an indiscriminate assemblage of bits and pieces in which nothing is of more value than anything else'); violence in books and films – when Bernard Levin alluded to psychological studies questioning the link between 'sado-pornographic *reading* and similar *doing*', Rees asked whether he would place much faith in such researches, 'if they assured him that a reading of *Der Stürmer* had no practical effect on those who carried out its sadistic recommendations'. (This said, Rees was predisposed to deplore any form of literary censorship; and he went into the dock in defence of *Last Exit to Brooklyn*.) Ardent cold warrior he might have been, but he could not comfortably be classified as of the Right or of the Left. The proponent of liberal values, he saw himself as standing in the western intellectual tradition, of dispassionate enquiry and unfettered debate ('reasonable men in reasonable discourse about common themes'). The flight from rationalism dismayed him – in the eyes of the counter-culture, the commitment to reason was the original sin of the West. Rees's fears for *Brief Encounters* were real – collections of articles rarely made good books and he had been badgered into compiling this one – but the reception was heartening. His essays were 'beautifully shaped and written, and lucidly argued' (Paul Bailey), demonstrating that 'vitality and reason can be allies rather than inevitable opponents' (*Observer*); Rees was his own man: 'it's a tribute that he can arouse disagreement in somebody so often on his side' (Julian Symonds, *Sunday Times*). Two backward-glancing essays were especially praised, one on the world of Lytton Strachey (importantly, homosexual, though this dimension has been overlooked), the other on Berlin in the

1920s, a reminder that behind the glamorous veil thrown over the epoch by cultural historians lies a rotting dung-heap of human suffering.

Rees kept up his column to the end, through the desolating loss of Margie in June 1976. 'Every minute of the day he missed my mother and his sorrow was so great that I knew there was nothing I could do for him', remembers their daughter Jenny Rees. Margie had succumbed to cancer, the disease which in November 1979 brought Goronwy himself to a strike-bound Charing Cross Hospital. There in his room friends and colleagues from *Encounter* held a party for his seventieth birthday. There were plans for a move to a nursing home not far from Oxford but on 12 December Rees died. Among old friends who visited him in hospital was Isaiah Berlin, and, by chance, it was Berlin's *Against the Current* that Rees had chosen as the subject of his very last *Encounter* column (October 1979). It is a teasing piece, inasmuch as it suggests a growing hospitality towards a view of life and the world at odds with the main current of classical western thought. Pondering Berlin's essays, Rees writes of

the belief that in direct experience and intuition human beings can achieve knowledge of a reality which is not accessible to reason, and may sometimes be in conflict with it. Experience, in this context includes everything which they absorb through the senses and the affections, through family and kinship, and through tradition, religion and the arts . . . This belief has no logical or rational foundation; yet it is this alone which ultimately gives meaning and significance to human life.

A common judgement on Rees as author is that he promised more than he achieved. In some ways this is true: as a novelist he disappointed himself, and outside the province of fiction he never did deliver the major book on the 1930s that surely was within him.[58] Nonetheless, in fictive autobiography he found his distinctive voice, and the achievements in this genre show how gifted a writer he was. As for Rees's career, there is again the sense of promise unfulfilled, of a self-destructiveness even, or, at best, a failure to turn to account the many excellent openings he created for himself. It was said that he squandered his talents: Rees knew the charge; he had heard it before, mostly made by academics, for whom no career was worth pursuing unless it promised financial security and fairly rapid success. 'Poor Connolly . . . all that cleverness, all that knowledge, all that sensibility, all that wit and malice which could have been employed in setting every common room in a roar' (*Encounter*, November 1973). But there was a world beyond the common room, as Rees learnt early on at All Souls: there success was traditionally measured by impact on the larger political and intellectual scene. And Rees should also be seen in the light of another pattern, that of the European literary intellectual, passionately immersed in the life of the times: the many-sided Malraux figure, man of letters, man of action, adventurer, possessed of a streak of daring beneath the social poise. Rees invited no immodest comparisons but in one respect he measured up. He was truly a man of his age, alive to all its hopes and its tragedies. It is certainly not difficult to believe John Morgan when that journalist and broadcaster writes of Rees: 'Of all the eminent Welshmen I've known, he was the most fascinating and, in terms of the conflicts of our century, the most important in his interests.'[59]

Notes

1   National Library of Wales (NLW), Calvinistic Methodist Archives, R. J. Rees Manuscripts, MS 22844.

2   Quoted in Jenny Rees, *Looking for Mr Nobody: The Secret Life of Goronwy Rees* (London: Weidenfeld & Nicolson, 1994), p. 257.

3   Jack Wanger, interview with John Harris, 15 May 1994.

4   Ibid.

5   Goronwy Rees, 'Memories of New College, 1928–31', in John Buxton and Penry Williams (eds.), *New College, Oxford: 1379–1979* (Oxford: Warden and Fellows of New College, 1979), p. 121.

6   Sir Richard Wilberforce, letter to Jenny Rees, 2 May 1995; the Crossman quotation in this paragraph is from his review of *A Chapter of Accidents*, *New Statesman*, 25 February 1972, and the Rowse from the chapter on Rees and Elizabeth Bowen in his *Memories and Glimpses* (London: Methuen, 1986).

7   Goronwy Rees, letter, 2 July 1931 (private collection).

8   Letter to Maire Lynd, 6 September 1931.

9   A. J. Ayer, *Part of My Life* (London: Collins, 1977), pp. 107–8.

10 From an undated letter to Douglas Jay; the Merthyr visit took place in September 1931.

11 'The Colliers', *Oxford Outlook*, 11, 56 (November 1931), 199. Rees published poems and reviews in *Oxford Outlook* (edited at this time by Isaiah Berlin), *New Oxford Outlook* (1933–4) and in the short-lived undergraduate journal *Farrago* (1930–1).

12 Sasha is taken to be Hamish St Clair Erskine, second son of the Earl of Rosslyn. He was sent down from New College at the end of Michaelmas Term, 1930.

13 Quoted in Shiela Grant Duff, *The Parting of Ways: A Personal Account of the Thirties* (London: Peter Owen, 1982), p. 44.

14 Goronwy Rees, 'A winter in Berlin: Part 2', *Planet*, 112 (1995), 34.

15 Letter to Shiela Grant Duff, September 1934.

16 Benny Morris, *The Roots of Appeasement: The British Weekly Press and Nazi Germany During the 1930s* (London: Frank Cass, 1991), p. 5.

17 From a letter to Shiela Grant Duff, quoted in *The Parting of Ways*, p. 64.

18 *Beyond the Dyke* (radio broadcast), June 1938, NLW, BBC (Wales) Archive, Scripts.

19 'From a Welshman abroad', *Bookman*, November 1934, 105–6.

20 'What then must we do?', *Spectator*, 12 March 1937, 480 (review of George Orwell, *The Road to Wigan Pier*).

21 'The left wing orthodoxy', *New Verse*, 31/32 (1938), 13; the subsequent MacNeice quotation is from his *The Strings Are False: An Unfinished Autobiography* (London: Faber & Faber, 1965), pp. 168–9.

22 Goronwy Rees, *Encounter*, September 1977, 52 (review of Martin Green, *Children of the Sun*).

23 'In defence of Welsh nationalism', *Spectator*, 10 September 1937, 416–17; Rees advanced the nationalist position in two radio broadcasts, *Beyond the Dyke*, June 1938.

24 *Welsh Nationalist*, October 1938, 1.

25 Letter to Keidrych Rhys, August 1937, NLW MS 22745D.

26 *Beyond the Dyke* (radio broadcast), June 1938.

27 Review of Christopher Isherwood, *The Memorial*, *Oxford Outlook*, 12, 58 (May 1932), 139–42.

28 Diana Trilling, 'Goronwy – and others: a remembrance of England', *Partisan Review*, January 1996, 24.

29 'Letter from a soldier', *Horizon*, July 1940, 467–71.

30 Four letters from Rees to Lehmann, 1940–1, are reprinted as an appendix to the paperback edition of Jenny Rees, *Looking for Mr Nobody* (1997). They first appeared in *New Welsh Review*, 29 (1995), 26–30.

31 Partly quoted in Noël Annan, *Changing Enemies: The Defeat and Regeneration of Germany* (London: HarperCollins, 1995), p. 152. A fuller text appears in M. E. Pelly and H. J. Yasamee (eds.), *Documents on British Policy Overseas*, Vol. 5 (London: HMSO, 1990), pp. 128–9.

32 His speech was reported at length in the *Manchester Guardian*, 3 August 1946, 6.

33 *Returning to Wales*, (radio broadcast), 28 September 1953, NLW, BBC (Wales) Archive, Scripts.

34 The lecture was published as *On the Use and Misuse of Universities* (Aberystwyth: University College of Wales, 1953).

35 Published as 'Predicaments', in *Welsh Anvil / Yr Einion*, 7 (1955), 18–31.

36 *Heterosexual Dictatorship: Male Homosexuality in Post War Britain* (London: Fourth Estate, 1996).

37   Interviewed by Rhys David, *Western Mail*, 9 February 1972.

38   *TLS*, 7 December 1979, 85 (review of Andrew Boyle, *The Climate of Treason*).

39   *Spectator*, 23 January 1948, 101–2 (review of Leopold Schwarzschild, *The Red Prussian: the life and legend of Karl Marx*).

40   *TLS*, 11 February 1972, 142 (review of *A Chapter of Accidents*).

41   *Listener*, 22 January 1959, 180.

42   The McInnes review appeared in *Encounter*, October 1959, and the Compton Burnett in December 1959.

43   *The End of the Road* was broadcast 12 and 14 November 1959.

44   *The Auden Generation: Literature and Politics in England in the 1930s* (London: Bodley Head, 1976), p. 322.

45   *Welsh Nation*, April 1964, 3; reprinted in Meic Stephens (ed.), *Harri Webb: A Militant Muse: Selected Literary Journalism* (Bridgend: Seren, 1998), pp. 48–53.

46   *London Magazine*, December 1962, 74.

47   The early history of *Encounter* is well covered in Neil Berry, '*Encounter*', *London Magazine*, February–March 1995, 42–60.

48   *Encounter*, October 1973, 62.

49   In the *Spectator*, 12 February, O'Brien protested at Rees's review of 22 January, to which Rees replied, 19 February. Rees had first written on Chambers in the *Spectator*, 20 February 1953, and he returned to him again in the *Atlantic*, August 1967.

50   Hugh Trevor-Roper, *Sunday Times*, 13 February 1972; Michael Foot, *Evening Standard*, 15 February 1972; Geoffrey Grigson, *Country Life*, 17 February 1972; Philip Toynbee, *Observer*, 13 February 1972; Richard Crossman, *New Statesman*, 25 February 1972; Noël Annan, *TLS*, 11 February 1972.

51   For example, March 1969, June 1970, July 1972, August 1973, July 1977, July 1978, January 1979.

52   *Encounter*, November 1975, 44.

53   *London Magazine*, June–July 1972, 160 (review of *A Chapter of Accidents*).

54   October 1974; Rees also discussed Solzhenitsyn, in his columns for May 1970, January, March 1971, November 1972, September 1975, May, September 1976, September 1978.

55   May 1968; reprinted as 'America looks at itself', in *Brief Encounters* (London: Chatto & Windus, 1974), pp. 87–94.

56   'Goronwy – and others', 28–9.

57   See especially January 1974 and September 1976.

58 In August 1973 Michael Joseph agreed an advance of £2,000 for just such a book, to be entitled *In the Thirties*.

59 From a *Western Mail* article, 20 January 1987, reprinted in John Morgan, *John Morgan's Wales: A Personal Anthology* (Swansea: Christopher Davies, 1993), pp. 47–51.

Select Bibliography

Goronwy Rees: books authored, edited, and translated

The Summer Flood (London: Faber & Faber, 1932).

A Bridge to Divide Them (London: Faber & Faber, 1937).

Danton's Death: A Play in Four Acts, by Georg Büchner; translated by Stephen Spender and Goronwy Rees (London: Faber & Faber, 1939).

Where No Wounds Were (London: Chatto & Windus, 1950).

On the Use and Misuse of Universities (Aberystwyth: University College of Wales, 1953).

Conversations with Kafka: Notes and Reminiscences by Gustav Janouch, translated with a preface by Goronwy Rees (London: Derek Verschoyle, 1953; second edition, revised and enlarged: London: André Deutsch, 1971).

Thomas Jones, CH, MA, LLD, 1870–1955: President, University College of Wales, Aberystwyth, 1944–1954 (Aberystwyth: National Library of Wales, 1956).

A Bundle of Sensations (London: Chatto & Windus, 1960).

The Multi-Millionaires: Six Studies in Wealth (London: Weidenfeld & Nicolson, 1961).

The Rhine (London: Weidenfeld & Nicolson, 1967).

St Michael: A History of Marks and Spencer (London: Weidenfeld & Nicolson, 1969; revised edition: London: Pan Books, 1973).

The Great Slump: Capitalism in Crisis, 1929–33 (London: Weidenfeld & Nicolson, 1970).

A Chapter of Accidents (London: Chatto & Windus, 1972).

Brief Encounters (London: Chatto & Windus, 1974).

McVicar, John, *McVicar by Himself*, edited with an introduction by Goronwy Rees (London: Hutchinson, 1974).

Dalgety: The History of a Merchant House (n.d., privately printed for the directors).

Goronwy Rees: Sketches in Autobiography, edited with introduction and notes by John Harris (Cardiff: University of Wales Press, 2001).

Reprint of *A Bundle of Sensations* and *A Chapter of Accidents*, with the essay, 'A winter in Berlin'.

Goronwy Rees: contributions to books and periodicals

No full-scale bibliography of Rees yet exists; below are the principal items used in preparing this study.

'From a Welshman abroad', *Bookman*, November 1934, 105–6.

'The empirical society', *Spectator*, 13 December 1935, 992. Review of Sidney and Beatrice Webb, *Soviet Communism*.

'The hollow man', *Spectator*, 20 March 1936, 522–4. Review of Konrad Heiden, *Hitler*.

'What then must we do?', *Spectator*, 12 March 1937, 480. Review of George Orwell, *The Road to Wigan Pier*.

'The Russian mystery', *Spectator*, 18 June 1937, 1132.

'In defence of Welsh nationalism', *Spectator*, 10 September 1937, 416–17.

'In the valley', *Spectator*, 5 November 1937, 806–7. Review of James Hanley, *Grey Children: A Study of Humbug and Misery in South Wales*.

Beyond the Dyke, two BBC Wales broadcasts, June 1938; partly reprinted in Patrick Hannan (ed.), *Wales on the Wireless: A Broadcasting Anthology* (Llandysul: Gomer, 1988).

'Bolshevism and the West', *Spectator*, 9 September 1938, 397–8. Review of F. Borkenau, *The Communist International*.

'Hitler and Bismarck', *Spectator*, 17 February 1939, 248–9.

'Two birthdays', *Spectator*, 21 April 1939, 657–8. On Hitler and Charlie Chaplin.

'Letter from a soldier', *Horizon*, July 1940, 467–71.

'Germany's part in European recovery', *Manchester Guardian*, 3 August 1946, 6. Report of Rees's address to a Liberal summer school.

'The informer and the communist', *Spectator*, 20 February 1953, 206–7. On Whittaker Chambers and Alger Hiss.

Returning to Wales, BBC Wales broadcast, 28 September 1953; partly reprinted in Patrick Hannan (ed.), *Wales on the Wireless: A Broadcasting Anthology* (Llandysul: Gomer, 1988).

'Preface', in *The Answers of Ernst von Salomon to the 131 Questions in the Allied Military Government 'Fragebogen'*, trans. Constantine Fitzgibbon (London: Putnam, 1954), vii–xii.

'Predicaments', *Welsh Anvil / Yr Einion*, 7 (1955), 18–31. Text of lecture delivered July 1954.

'Guy Burgess stripped bare!', *People*, 11 March 1956, 5. Continued: 18 March, 3; 25 March, 3; 1 April, 3; 8 April, 10.

'From another country', *New Statesman*, 24 February 1961, 296, 298. On Wales.

Review of Michael Foot, *Aneurin Bevan, Vol. 1: 1897–1945*, London *Magazine*, December 1962, 74–7.

'Have the Welsh a future?', *Encounter*, March 1964, 3–13.

'Diary: from Berlin to Munich', *Encounter*, April 1964, 3–12.

'The horsemen', *London Magazine*, April 1964, 8–31. Story.

'A visa for Kafka', *Encounter*, September 1964, 27–34.

'The witness', *Spectator*, 22 January 1965, 105. Review of Whittaker Chambers, *Cold Friday*. Response, 12 February (Conor Cruise O'Brien); reply, 19 February (GR).

'A Welsh elegy', *Spectator*, 14 May 1965, 641. Review of Emyr Humphreys, *Outside the House of Baal*.

[André Malraux], *Encounter*, January 1968, 52–3.

[Twentieth anniversary of *Encounter*], *Encounter*, October 1973, 4.

[Were the intellectuals duped?], *Encounter*, January 1974, 25–7.

[Solzhenitsyn, *The Gulag Archipelago*], *Encounter*, October 1974, 39–42.

'Darkness at Noon and "Grammatical Fiction" ', in Harold Harris (ed.), *Astride Two Cultures: Arthur Koestler at 70* (London: Hutchinson, 1975), 102–22.

[Writers of the thirties], *Encounter*, September 1976, 50–2.

'Back to the Boathouse', *TLS*, 29 April 1977, 505. Review of Paul Ferris, *Dylan Thomas*, and Daniel Jones, *My Friend Dylan Thomas*.

'On intellectual reviews', *Encounter*, October 1978, 3–10.

'Memories of New College, 1928–31', in John Buxton and Penry Williams (eds.), *New College, Oxford, 1379–1979* (Oxford: Warden and Fellows of New College, 1979), 120–6.

'A winter in Berlin', *Planet*, 111 (1995), 13–24; continued 112 (1995), 29–39; reprinted in John Harris (ed.), *Goronwy Rees: Sketches in Autobiography* (Cardiff: University of Wales Press, 2001).

Goronwy Rees: biography and criticism

Books

Annan, Noël, *Our Age: Portrait of a Generation* (London: Weidenfeld & Nicolson, 1990), 224–44 ('The Cambridge spies').

—, *Changing Enemies: The Defeat and Regeneration of Germany* (London: HarperCollins, 1995).

Ayer, A. J. , *Part of My Life* (London: Collins, 1977).

—, *More of My Life* (London: Collins, 1984).

Grant Duff, Shiela, *The Parting of Ways: A Personal Account of the Thirties* (London: Peter Owen, 1982). With much on Rees, including passages from his letters.

Hamilton, Nigel, *Monty: The Making of a General, 1887–1942* (London: H. Hamilton, 1981).

Harris, John, 'Introduction' and 'Goronwy Rees: the memoirist', in John Harris (ed.), *Goronwy Rees: Sketches in Autobiography* (Cardiff: University of Wales Press, 2001).

Higgins, Patrick, *Heterosexual Dictatorship: Male Homosexuality in Post War Britain* (London: Fourth Estate, 1996).

Hynes, Samuel, *The Auden Generation: Literature and Politics in England in the 1930s* (London: Bodley Head, 1976).

Ignatieff, Michael, *Isaiah Berlin: A Life* (London: Chatto & Windus, 1998).

MacNeice, Louis, *The Strings Are False: An Unfinished Autobiography* (London: Faber & Faber, 1965).

Morgan, John, *John Morgan's Wales: A Personal Anthology* (Swansea: Christopher Davies, 1993), 47–51 ('Goronwy Rees'). Partly based on conversations with Rees.

Morris, Benny, *The Roots of Appeasement: The British Weekly Press and Nazi Germany During the 1930s* (London: Frank Cass, 1991).

Rees, Jenny, *Looking for Mr Nobody: The Secret Life of Goronwy Rees* (London: Weidenfeld & Nicholson, 1994). Paperback edn (London: Phoenix, 1997) with appendix reproducing four letters from Rees to Rosamond Lehmann (previously printed in *New Welsh Review*, 29, 1995). US edn (Brunswick: Transaction, 2000) with 'Introduction: Goronwy – and others: a remembrance of England', by Diana Trilling, pp. xi–xlvii.

Rowse, A. L., *Memories and Glimpses* (London: Methuen, 1986), 417–32 ('Elizabeth Bowen; Goronwy Rees').

—, *All Souls in My Lifetime* (London: Duckworth, 1993).

West, Nigel and Oleg Tsarev, *The Crown Jewels: The British Secrets at the Heart of the KGB Archives* (London: HarperCollins, 1998).

Periodical articles, book reviews

Annan, Noël, 'Burgess: scamp into scoundrel', *Times Literary Supplement*, 11 February 1972, 142. Review of *A Chapter of Accidents*.

Ayer, A. J., 'Goronwy Rees', *The Times*, 14 December 1979, 16. Obituary notice.

—, 'Goronwy Rees', *Encounter*, January 1981, 27–9.

Connolly, Cyril, 'A Welshman in search of a father', *Sunday Times*, 17 July 1960, 25. Review of *A Bundle of Sensations*.

Conquest, Robert, 'Corridors of impotence', *London Magazine*, June–July 1972, 157–60. Review of *A Chapter of Accidents*.

Crossman, Richard, 'Pleading from the grave', *New Statesman*, 25 February 1972, 242–3. Review of *A Chapter of Accidents*.

Ellis, E. L., 'The man of *The People*: Goronwy Rees and the Aberystwyth episode', *New Welsh Review*, 29 (1995), 44–7.

Footman, David, 'Goronwy Rees', *Encounter*, January 1981, 31–3.

Harris, John, 'Any one there? In search of Goronwy Rees', *Planet*, 110 (1995), 14–21.

—, 'A journalist in the thirties', *New Welsh Review*, 29 (1995), 31–8.

Jones, Richard, 'Fiction which foreshadows foolishness', *New Welsh Review*, 29 (1995), 39–43.

McCormick, Donald ('Richard Deacon'), 'Goronwy Rees', *Encounter*, January 1981, 30–1.

Morgan, John, 'Goronwy Rees', *Encounter*, January 1981, 33–5.

Norton-Taylor, Richard, 'Both perfect prey and perfect foil', *New Welsh Review*, 29 (1995), 48–50. On Rees as spy.

Power, Jonathan, 'Goronwy Rees', *Encounter*, January 1981, 35–6.

Rees, Jenny, 'The end of the affair', *New Welsh Review*, 29 (1995), 26–9. On Rees and Rosamond Lehmann, reproducing four letters by Rees.

Rogers, Timothy, 'Fragments of the self', *Times Literary Supplement*, 19 August 1960, 531. Review of *A Bundle of Sensations*.

Spender, Stephen, 'The left wing orthodoxy', *New Verse*, 31/32 (1938), 12–16.

Trilling, Diana, 'Goronwy – and others: a remembrance of England', *Partisan Review*, January 1996, 11–47.

Webb, Harri, 'Has Goronwy Rees a future?', *Welsh Nation*, April 1964, 3; reprinted in Meic Stephens (ed.), *Harri Webb: A Militant Muse: Selected Literary Journalism* (Bridgend: Seren, 1998), 48–53.

Non-printed sources

Jones, Thomas, Letter to Violet Markham, 4 August 1953, NLW, Dr Thomas Jones, CH, Collection, Class T, Vol. 9.

Rees, Goronwy, 'Beyond the Dyke' (June 1938), 'Returning to Wales' (September 1953), 'A Child in the Chapel' (January 1955) (radio scripts). BBC Written Archives Centre, Reading; National Library of Wales (NLW), Aberystwyth.

—, Letters to Shiela Grant Duff, Douglas Jay, T. Mervyn Jones and Maire Lynd. Private collections.

—, Letters to R. J. Rees. Calvinistic Methodist Archives, NLW MSS 24568–98.

—, Letter to Keidrych Rhys, August 1937, NLW MS 22745D.

—, 'Goronwy Rees: A Man of His Time', HTV Wales, 1978 [television interview with John Morgan]. NLW, Aberystwyth.

Rees, R. J., Scrapbook. Calvinistic Methodist Archives, NLW MS 22844.

Reilly, Sir Patrick, Letter to Jenny Rees, 27 January 1993. Private collection.

Wanger, Jack, Interview with John Harris, 15 May 1994.

Wilberforce, Sir Richard, Letter to Jenny Rees, 2 May 1995. Private collection.

[Willink Report] *Report of the University College of Wales, Aberystwyth, Committee of Enquiry, 1956–1957* (1957). University of Wales, Aberystwyth.

Index

Note: GR in the index stands for Goronwy Rees; page references in italic refer to illustrations; 'n.' indicates an endnote citation.